BLACK'S NATURE GUIDES

TREES
OF BRITAIN AND EUROPE

Margot and Roland Spohn

Contents

Tree and Shrub Species

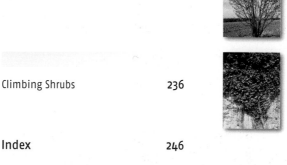

How to Use this Book

For each tree or shrub described in this book, you will find details of the habitat, as well as interesting facts on usage, history or biology. Informative illustrations with notes on key features make species easy to identify. The main photograph on each page shows the typical appearance of a particular tree. For some shrubs, which are often similar, the main photograph shows a typical section of the shrub. Other illustrations provide details of key features, which can help you to identify the trees and shrubs. Each margin contains text and images giving habitat details, important facts to note and a typical leaf. Trees and shrubs that are described on a whole page also feature a 'Did you know?' box providing the most interesting facts about the species.

Height: Height of growth above ground level in metres. **Month:** Main flowering season.

General information
This section provides interesting information from all kinds of areas, such as usage, history, medicine and biology.

The **small illustrations** show sections of the tree or shrub, which are important for identification purposes. These may be flowers, fruits or bark. The captions draw your attention to typical features.

For trees, a **main photograph** gives an impression of the whole tree. For shrubs, the photographs show either the whole shrub or a typical section. The captions refer to key features.

Hors
Aesculus h
H 15–35m Ap

Gardeners
in Europe s
only grew i
Nowadays v
has become
gardens. In t
rendered les
cooking oil a
used to feed
(hence the na
used for gam
weak veins ar
also contain e

crown rounded
off at top

...estnut

...stanum (horse-chestnut family)

...en planting this tree
...5. To begin with it
...parks and avenues.
...hade-giving crown, it
...pically found in beer
...need, the seeds were
...nd used to make
...Even the Turks
...s to their horses
...wadays they are
...Some drugs for
...leg syndrome
...rom them.

flowers up to
2cm in size

white with
yellow or red
markings

upright
spherical
flower stem

heavily spined

spherical fruit capsule,
up to 6cm in size

shiny, dark
brown seeds

broad crown

Habitat *Naturally
occurring in the
Balkans. Cultivated on
roadsides, squares and
in parks of central and
western Europe. Seeds
dispersed in September
and October.*

> emerging leaves have
> thick woolly hairs
> buds very sticky,
> especially at the end
> of winter
> popular tree for beer
> gardens

leaf
palmately
compound

leaflets
broadest in
top third

5–7 unstemmed
leaflets up to
20cm long

155

protruding branches,
branches of older
trees overhang

Did you know?

*Small larvae can be
seen using backlit
photography on the
brown spots that often
appear on the leaves. As
a result, the leaves fall
off. The larvae are those
of the Horse Chestnut
leaf miner, a moth that
first appeared in Europe
in 1984 and has since
become extremely
widespread.*

Habitat
The text describes the
tree or shrub's native
origin. For European
species, it also mentions
the natural habitat and
distribution in Europe.
For species that are not
native to Europe, the
text gives details of
where the tree or shrub
is popularly grown.
Typical features of the
tree or shrub are also
described and shown
in a small photograph
above.

Key features
A summary of essential
information, for examp-
le, about identification,
distribution or usage.

Leaf
An illustration of a
typical leaf, highlighting
important identifying
features in the leaf area.

Colour code
Each of the four main
groups is marked with
the relevant colour (see
the front flap of the
book).

Symbol
The silhouette allows
the leaf shapes to be
classified further (see the
front flap of the book).

'Did you know?' box
The box contains interesting information on the
tree or shrub, and is
often accompanied by a
picture. In many cases, a
key related species is
also featured.

Identifying Typical Forms

The trees and shrubs in this book are assigned to main groups according to their forms, such as coniferous or deciduous. These groups can be recognised quickly using the colour code. The form can usually be identified from a distance. It gives an initial impression of the tree and thus the first clue to its identity.

Trees belonging to one particular form have basic common features:

Spruce

Maple

Conifers have one main trunk and a crown, which is usually evergreen and often conical.

Deciduous trees have one main trunk and a crown, which is usually bare in winter and is often spherical or uneven in shape.

Hazel

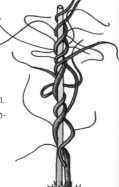

Chinese Wisteria

Climbing shrubs cannot stand upright on their own. They need a climbing aid to attach themselves to or coil around.

Shrubs have multiple stems, often of equal strength, which arise from the base.

The Structure of a Tree

For identification purposes, it is important to be able to recognise the typical structure of a tree. To do so, we can differentiate between the various parts of a tree: The **trunk** emerges directly out of the ground from a system of underground roots. It may reach as far as the top of the tree, split into several trunks – often of an equal strength – above the ground, or be fairly short. From the trunk emerge a number of **branches**, which divide into **twigs**. Branches and twigs together form the **crown**, the highest part of which is known as the **treetop**.

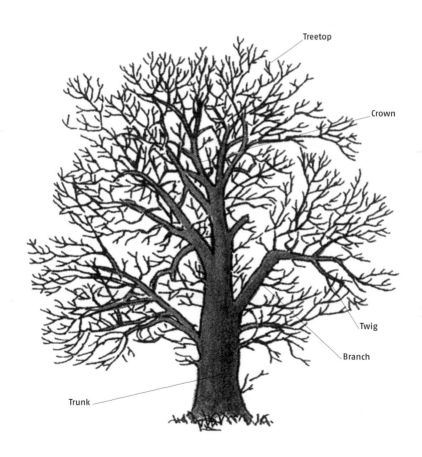

Treetop

Crown

Twig

Branch

Trunk

Leaves

Leaf features are some of the most important identifying characteristics of a tree. The main groups of trees in this book are divided into subgroups with five silhouettes which can be found in the colour bars. The silhouettes symbolise the different shapes of leaf blade and margin. Along with the appearance of the individual leaf (**leaf shapes**), the way in which the leaves are attached to the twig can also be important for identification purposes (**leaf attachment**).

Four leaf attachments

Leaves emerge along the twigs in a few basic patterns. For identification purposes, it is extremely useful to recognise these patterns. To do so, you must examine a section of the twig that is closer to the branch than the tip of the twig.

Most leaves are attached to the twigs as follows:

Leaf Structure

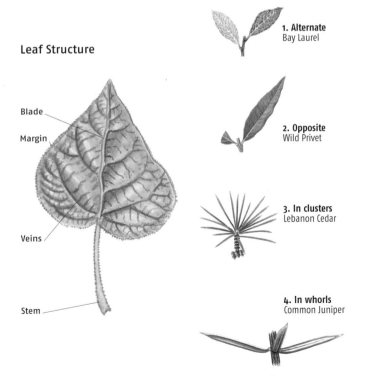

Blade

Margin

Veins

Stem

1. Alternate
Bay Laurel

2. Opposite
Wild Privet

3. In clusters
Lebanon Cedar

4. In whorls
Common Juniper

Five leaf shapes

Each of the five silhouettes is given in the colour bar on the relevant identification page.

1. Needle-shaped or scalated leaves

Needles
Sitka Spruce

Scalated leaves
Mediterranean Cypress

2. Lobed leaves

Lobed margin
English Oak

Three-lobed leaf
Montpellier Maple

3. Undivided, flat leaves with a smooth leaf margin

Oval
Common Beech

Heart-shaped
Judas Tree

Lanceolate
Mezereon

4. Undivided, flat leaves with a crenate, toothed or serrated margin

Serrated margin
Wild Cherry

Crenate margin
Antarctic Beech

Toothed margin
English Holly

5. Compound leaves

Pinnate
Mastic Tree

Odd-pinnate
Common Walnut

Bi-pinnate
Pink Siris

Trifoliate
Japanese Bitter Orange

Palmately divided
Horse Chestnut

Major Flower Shapes

Many trees and shrubs form typical flowers, which make excellent identifying features. The way in which the flowers are attached to the twigs is also important. Some flowers stand singly, while others form characteristically structured groups. It is also worthwhile noting the flowering season: flowers often appear in spring before the leaves.

Flower structure

The flower silhouette shows the basic structure of a flower. Trees and shrubs have countless variants and in many cases whole parts may be missing.

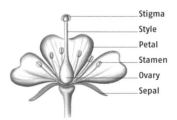

Stigma
Style
Petal
Stamen
Ovary
Sepal

Male flower just with stamens and no ovaries
Castor Oil Plant

Female flower just with ovaries and stigmas, but no stamens
Castor Oil Plant

Flower shape

The individual parts of a flower can exist in varying numbers, attachments and shapes so flowers come in a wide range of different appearances.

Four petals
English Holly

Five petals
Chinese Quince

Numerous petals
Kobus Magnolia

Densely packed
Double-flowering Almond Tree

Pea-like flower
Spanish Broom

Salverform
Angel's Trumpet

Funnelform
Cape Leadwort

Bell-shaped
Tree Heath

Flower attachment

Flowers do not just appear singly on twigs, but often form groups with individual flowers attached in different ways.

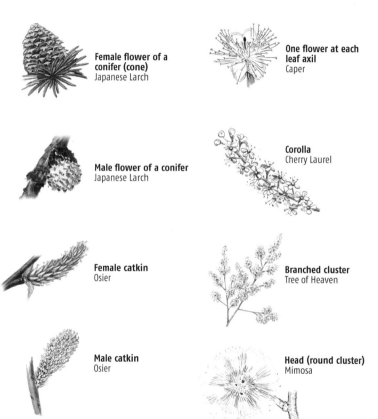

Female flower of a conifer (cone)
Japanese Larch

One flower at each leaf axil
Caper

Male flower of a conifer
Japanese Larch

Corolla
Cherry Laurel

Female catkin
Osier

Branched cluster
Tree of Heaven

Male catkin
Osier

Head (round cluster)
Mimosa

Major Fruits

Fruit trees are cultivated solely for their fruit. But fruits can also make other types of tree and shrub easier to identify. It is therefore worth looking out for them on unknown trees or shrubs. Fruits begin developing immediately after the flowering stage and can often be found in varying degrees of ripeness over a long period of time. In many cases, fruits may even be found in winter on bare trees or hidden among the leaves below.

Coniferous trees

Cones
Pine

The seeds nestle between mostly dry, woody scales.

Berry-like cones
Common Juniper

Fleshy scales surround the seeds.

Deciduous trees

Capsule fruits
Horse Chestnut

The ripe fruit opens and releases a quantity of seeds.

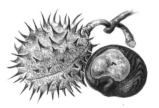

Pods
Scotch Broom

The typical fruit of pea-like flowering trees opens along two seams.

Berries
Gooseberry

The seeds are embedded in juicy fruit flesh inside the ripe fruit.

Stone fruits
Plum

A fairly thick fruit flesh surrounds a hard stone in which the seed is enclosed.

Nuts
Hazel

The seed is enclosed in a hard shell without any flesh.

Fruits in woody cups
Cork Oak

The fruit sits inside a special cup (acorn) instead of directly on a twig.

Winged fruits (samaras)
Manna Ash

The fruit consists of one part, which contains the seeds, and another seedless, wing-like part.

Compound fruits
Wild Raspberry

At first glance, this kind of fruit looks like a single fruit. However, it is actually made up of many small individual fruits (or stone fruits in the case of the Wild Raspberry).

'Did you know?' Boxes

We come into contact with trees and their products every day, but we do not usually spare them a thought. This book therefore presents interesting facts about each tree and shrub from all kinds of different fields. In the case of species that are given a whole page, the interesting facts take up the most space. A '**Did you know?**' box then also highlights particularly interesting information.

Trees as providers of raw materials

The most important part of a tree is its wood. Wood often played a vital role in mankind's survival throughout history. Today, we still use it as fuel, a building material and raw material to make paper. Wood can have very different characteristics, depending on the tree of origin. Wood experts can thus choose the most suitable material for each type of use.

Trees as providers of food and medicines

Fruit trees and shrubs grow in almost every large kitchen garden. Apples, in particular, are one of the most popular types of fruit and come in a large range of different varieties. Wild fruit, gathered from wild-growing shrubs and trees, is also gaining more popularity. However, trees also supply important raw substances for plant-based medicines. Some trees are therefore cultivated in large numbers.

Did you know?

The fruits of the Cornelian Cherry are known as 'Dirndln' in Austria, like the traditional dress, and are a real insider tip for lovers of wild fruit. Jams made from the ripe, sour fruits have a similar flavour to woodland strawberries and rose hips.

Did you know?

Yew wood is heavy, hard and yet highly flexible. Even 'Ötzi', the Stone Age man found in an Alpine glacier, had a bow made of Yew with him. In the Middle Ages, people used Yew wood to make cross-bows and measuring tools and for woodturning work.

Curative ingredients are found in different parts of trees. Depending on the type of tree or shrub, drug manufacturers may require the fruits, leaves, bark, or occasionally the flowers or wood. The harvesting and gathering of these elements is often a manual task. To retain the active ingredients, the processing must be carried out with great care.

Ornamental trees

These days, hardly any garden owners think about the origins of the many beautifully blooming or brightly coloured trees and shrubs on which they lavish so much care. We are also impressed by the wide variety of often foreign trees and shrubs in parks. Countless ornamental forms, which have been cultivated from the original wild forms, can also be frequently seen.

Did you know?

*The distinctive coloured caterpillar of the Privet Hawk-moth (*Sphinx ligustri*) occasionally feeds on the bush. It is a nocturnally active butterfly.*

Symbolism and legends

Whether searching for food or shelter or gathering building materials or dyestuffs, our ancestors dealt with trees almost on a daily basis. In pre-historic times, men were particularly impressed by trees that they had to look up to and that were a good deal older than them. They held gatherings beneath the trees, consecrated them to the gods or described them in their mythologies and legends. Exciting anecdotes and stories abound about countless trees.

Did you know?

Box trees can easily be pruned into orna-mental features and figures and were therefore very popular during the Renaissance and Baroque periods. The custom to use Box to edge garden beds dates back to the Romans, who originally brought this tradition to western and central Europe.

Trees as habitats

Cleared, man-made landscapes offer wild animals and plants little in the way of a habitat, and usually support very few species. This is why conservationists try to maintain or re-establish diverse environments with hedgerows, copses and forests. Trees provide a habitat for many animals – from red deer to aphids – as well as for fungi, mosses and flowers.

Did you know?

In Greek mythology, Hercules had to obtain the golden apples of the Hesperides as one of his twelve labours. He completed the task and received golden quinces as a reward. In fact, the 'Apple of Venus' was in reality a quince.

Silver Fir

Abies alba (pine family)
H 30–50m May

male flowers at ends of shoots

To make their tangy fir honey, bees do not visit the trees' flowers. Instead, they gather the sugary honeydew excreted by various parasites, which live on fir and spruce trees. The Silver Fir population has declined drastically over the past 200 years. It was one of the first species of tree to be noticeably affected by increasing air pollution, becoming the most well-known tree of the forest dieback phenomenon.

Habitat *In the mountains of central and southern Europe, often with the Norway Spruce (p. 25) or Common Beech (p. 60). Characteristic, light grey bark.*

> **can live to around 600 yrs**
> **roots reach deep down into the ground**
> **supplies non-resinous wood**

tree top pointed on young trees, rounded on old trees

form slender and conical

tip round or crenate

glossy dark green above

2 white bands below

needles flexible, up to 3cm long

female flowers cone-shaped, upright

branches horizontal, often differing in length

cones erect, around 1cm long

scales with fine tips

18

needles arranged on the sides so twigs are flat

Did you know?

Cones found on the forest floor are never fir cones. These decompose on the trees once they have ripened. Their scales then fall to the ground, while the central cores remain on the branch.

Greek Fir

Abies cephalonica (pine family)
H 20–35m May

The Greek Fir is threatened by mankind in its natural habitat, suffering damage from over-intensive tourism and air pollution as well as forest fires. The species has therefore been included on the worldwide list of endangered tree species. Greece now has nature reserves to protect the tree.

Habitat Grows wild in forests in the mountains of Greece. In the rest of Europe, it is grown in parks and as an ornamental tree. Bark has many small platelets.

> early shoots prone to frost damage
> tolerates aridity in summer
> also cultivated as Christmas trees

trunk often forked at the top with irregularly spreading branches

form oval to broadly conical

cones upright, up to 14cm long

scales with folded back tips

needles arranged spirally around the twig

tip sharply pointed

needles stiff, up to 3.5cm long

2 narrow white bands below

White Fir

Abies concolor (pine family)
H 20–30m May–June

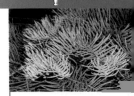

Anyone who has ever celebrated Christmas in California will probably have done so beneath a White Fir. These trees are grown in plantations to keep up with demand for the popular Christmas tree. The bark of young trees often forms blisters containing aromatic, transparent resin. This Canada balsam is used to embed microscopic specimens as if in glass.

Habitat Native to North America. In parks and gardens in central Europe. Needles mostly curved characteristically upwards on twig.

> attractive ornamental tree
> tolerates dry urban climates
> needs plenty of space in a garden

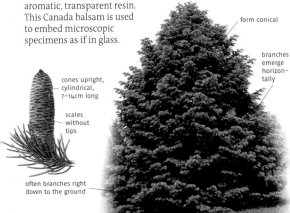

form conical

branches emerge horizontally

cones upright, cylindrical, 7–14cm long

scales without tips

often branches right down to the ground

bluish-green on both sides

needles flexible, 4–7cm long

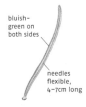

Grand Fir

Abies grandis (pine family)
H 30–50m May–June

Habitat *Native to the Pacific coast of North America. Found in parks and forests in Europe. Needles differing in length on same twig.*

> *largest species of Fir*
> *needles smell of tangerine when crushed*
> *needs plenty of humidity*

In its natural habitat, this fir can grow up to 100 metres tall. It tolerates frost well and grows fairly rapidly in suitable soils. This means it produces plenty of wood. However, the quality is not valuable so it is mainly used to make paper. Grand Firs also make attractive Christmas trees and decorative sprays.

upper branches splayed out diagonally

crown slender and conical

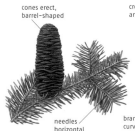

cones erect, barrel-shaped

needles horizontal

branches curved

needles flexible, 2.5–6cm long

2 white bands below

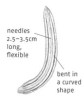

Noble Fir

Abies procera (pine family)
H 15–25m May

Habitat *Native to North America. Mostly in parks in Europe. Recognisable by its almost silvery needles, even without cones.*

> *most eye-catching cones of all the fir species*
> *also known as a 'Red Fir'*
> *can grow up to 80m tall in its native habitat*

The Noble Fir holds two records among fir trees: it forms the largest cones and lives the longest – over 700 years. The densely needled twigs make attractive, long-lasting advent wreaths. In gardens, the often gnarled-looking tree is robust, but not particularly ornamental.

form very sparse, often uneven

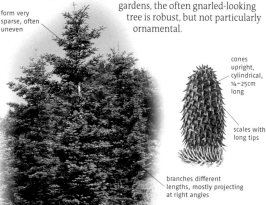

cones upright, cylindrical, 14–25cm long

scales with long tips

needles 2.5–3.5cm long, flexible

bent in a curved shape

branches different lengths, mostly projecting at right angles

Nordmann Fir

Abies nordmanniana (pine family)
H 25–60m May–June

In its natural habitat, this tree grows in mountainous regions with cool, not overly dry summers and extremely cold winters. It is more likely to suffer from dry heat in summer than from winter frosts. In general, however, it copes well with our climate. The soft, non-resinous wood is valued in its native lands for the manufacturing of pulp and paper.

Habitat *Naturally occurring from the Caucasus to north-east Turkey. In parks, gardens and forests in central Europe. Twigs often densely needled.*

> *needs damp soils*
> *can live up to 500 years in its native habitat*
> *needles remain on tree for many years*

male flowers long

tree top pointed

crown very even and conical

needles up to 3.5cm long

blunt or pointed

2 white bands below

21

scales with long tips

cones erect, up to 18cm long

mostly branches right down to the ground

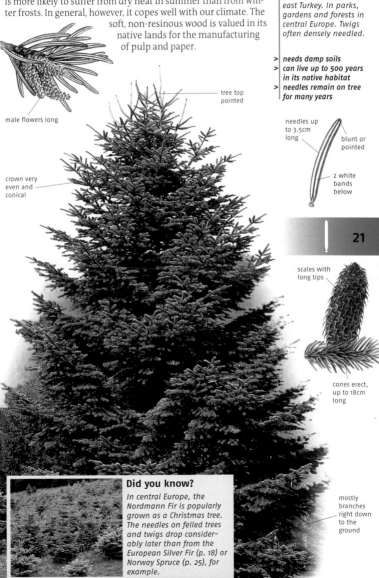

Did you know?

In central Europe, the Nordmann Fir is popularly grown as a Christmas tree. The needles on felled trees and twigs drop considerably later than from the European Silver Fir (p. 18) or Norway Spruce (p. 25), for example.

Korean Fir
Abies koreana (pine family)
H 5–10m May

Habitat Native to Korea. In parks and gardens in Europe. Forms many cones, even on lower branches.

> attractive ornamental tree
> tolerates urban climates well
> cultivars also available

Korean Firs grow extremely slowly. In their natural habitat, they grow up to 20 metres tall, but seldom reach more than seven metres in gardens. This means they are perfect for front and small gardens. Trees that are only one metre tall often have an abundance of cones which remain on the branches well into winter.

crown broadly conical

branches attached like storeys of a building

young cones a distinctive red-violet colour

needles 1–2cm long, flat

2 white bands below

blunt, crenate

cones erect, 5–7cm long

Spanish Fir
Abies pinsapo (pine family)
H 15–25m May

cone scales very dense

turn reddish-brown when

Habitat Only grows wild in southern Spain. Often found in parks and gardens in Europe. With their projecting needles, the twigs resemble brushes.

> rare and endangered in its native habitat
> needs plenty of sunshine
> also cultivated as a blue-green variety

Spain is trying to maintain the last natural forests where this fir grows, but this means battling against the constant forest fires, which can destroy stands but also create space for young growth. To make sure that clearings close faster, the Spanish plant young trees as well as relying on natural regeneration.

conic crown

cones upright, 10–15cm long

branches attached evenly, dense

needles 1–2cm long, blunt, rigid

base broad, shield-shaped

Douglas Fir

Pseudotsuga menziesii (pine family)
H 25–50m May

The Douglas Fir grows quickly and supplies hard, durable wood. It can yield twice as much timber as a Norway Spruce grown in the same location, so it is hardly surprising that it is one of the world's most economically important trees. The first seeds were brought to Europe in 1827 by the Scottish naturalist Douglas. Germany's Imperial Chancellor Count von Bismarck was particularly keen to cultivate them in Germany, ordering them to be planted in many sites from around 1880.

Habitat Native to western North America. Found in forests, gardens and parks in central Europe. Easily recognisable by its characteristic cones.

> needles smell of orange or lemon when crushed
> can grow to more than 100m tall in its natural habitat
> cones drop in one piece

conic crown

male flowers at ends of twigs

2 white bands below

needles 2–4cm long, soft, thin

dull, dark green above

23

branches in whorls

female flowers greenish, shaggy

cones hanging, 5–8 cm long

scales with 3 tips

straight trunk

Did you know?

The scaly bark of the Douglas Fir is distinctively thick. In its natural habitat, the bark protects the living trunk from frequent forest fires.

Canadian Hemlock
Tsuga canadensis (pine family)
H 10–30m May

cones oval,
1.5–2cm long

Habitat Native to
north-eastern North
America. In parks in
central and western
Europe, occasionally in
forests. The small cones
hang from the twigs.

> also grows extremely
well in the shade
> can be trimmed into a
hedge
> different garden
varieties well-known

The Canadian Hemlock yields large quantities of wood in
cool, damp climates. However, the wood is soft and does not last
long. In North America, it is therefore mainly used to make boxes
and paper. Crushed needles from the
tree smell similar to the poisonous
Hemlock plant.

leading shoot
often slightly
overhanging

crown mostly broad, uneven

some shorter needles on
the upper side of twig

2 white
bands
below

needles
1.2–1.8cm
long

rough
margin

female
flower

needles in 2 rows

24

Brewer's Spruce
Picea breweriana (pine family)
H 8–15m April–May

Habitat Native to the
United States, from
Oregon to northern
California. In gardens
in Europe. Side twigs
hang down like a mane.

> sensitive to air pollution
> only suitable for large
gardens
> also known as a
'Weeping Spruce'

Brewer's Spruce is the rarest species of American spruce found
in the wild. It was named after Professor Brewer who discovered
it in the second half of the 19th century. With its trailing twigs, it
has a highly decorative appearance
and is thus popularly planted as
a freestanding single tree in
parks and gardens.

twigs
hanging

main branches
flexible,
upswept

cones hanging,
10–12cm long

form
broadly
conical

needles
2–3.5cm
long,
flat

emerge from a
protuberance

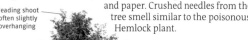

Norway Spruce

Picea abies (pine family)

H 25–50m May

female flowers erect

For a long time, Norway Spruce trees were mainly grown in dense monocultures where other plants found it almost impossible to thrive. However, pests like bark beetles are extremely widespread in these forests. Nowadays, the staple tree of the forestry industry is grown increasingly in mixed cultures with other trees – but it will be a long while before the last monotone forests disappear.

Habitat Native to northern Europe and the mountains of central Europe. Often found in forests in lower regions. Needles arranged around twigs.

> good-value Christmas tree
> needles drop slowly
> prefers humid, cool locations

even, conical crown

branches horizontal or curved upwards

needles up to 2.5cm long, sharply pointed

4-edged

emerge from a protuberance

straight, column-shaped trunk

cones hanging, up to 16cm long

young male flowers red

needles twisting around twig

Did you know?

Spruce trees have shallow roots: their main roots grow close to the surface instead of deep underground. This means that the trees can thrive in areas with little soil, but lose their stability easily during storms and may fall, together with their roots.

Oriental Spruce
Picea orientalis (pine family)
H 15–50m May

Habitat *Native to northern Asia Minor and the Caucasus. Often found in parks in Europe. The extremely short needles are a typical feature.*

> *also known as the 'Caucasian Spruce'*
> *cones similar to those of the Norway Spruce (p. 25)*
> *shortest needles of any Spruce tree*

In its native habitat, the Oriental Spruce can form dense forests. Its wood is highly resinous, which is why it was split into small pieces and used for lighting in the past. The same applied to pinewood chips from pine trees. The resin often oozes from the twigs in droplets.

cones hanging, up to 9cm long

branches project out or upwards

crown slender, even and conical

violet when unripe

mostly has branches down to the ground

dark green, highly glossy

blunt tip

needles 5–8mm long, 4-edged

Serbian Spruce
Picea omorika (pine family)
H 15–35 m May

male flowers orange initially, later turning yellow

needles spirally arranged around twig

Habitat *Native to Bosnia and Serbia. In gardens in Europe. The usually numerous cones are resinous.*

> *very undemanding*
> *tolerates smoke and soot*
> *one of the most common conifers in gardens*

Fossils prove that the Serbian Spruce was once considerably more widespread than it is now. Today, it only occurs naturally in one small area in barely accessible gorges. With its slender form and often hanging branches, it can cope well in snowy regions since the snow slides off the branches when it reaches a certain weight.

tree top pointed

crown very slender, conical or pillar-shaped

female flowers dark red

branches project outwards or in curves, short

needles up to 2cm long, flattened

2 light bands below

cones hanging, 3–6cm long

glossy brown

Blue Spruce

Picea pungens (pine family)
H 10–30m May–June

female flowers brownish-orange

The Blue Spruce is the state tree of the American states Utah and Colorado. Although the wood is not of a particularly good quality, the trees make excellent windbreaks. In Europe, the blue-green variety has provoked great interest among gardeners and is one of the most popular variants of conifer in private gardens.

crown even and conical

male flowers initially reddish, later turn yellow or light brown

branches rigid in dense whorls

cones hanging, 6–10cm long

light brown

Habitat Native to the central US states. Grown as an ornamental tree in central and northern Europe. Forms with bright bluish-green needles are especially popular.

> *also known as the 'Colorado Spruce'*
> *tolerates frost well*
> *widespread in many ornamental varieties*

sharply pointed

needles up to 3cm long

often curved

Dwarf Alberta Spruce

Picea glauca 'Conica' (pine family)
H 1.5–3 m April–May

The Dwarf Alberta Spruce is a natural mutant of the White Spruce, which is native to Canada. Its growth is highly restricted. The trees do not form any seeds and can thus only be propogated artificially. Occasionally, trees form normal branches with cones. However, seedlings taken from these grow into conventional White Spruce trees (*Picea glauca*) instead of Dwarf Alberta Spruce trees.

form very even, conical

twigs very dense

usually has branches down to the ground

Habitat Discovered in Canada in 1904. In gardens, parks, rockeries and cemeteries in Europe. The dense, young twigs are light green.

> *grows extremely slowly*
> *suitable for small gardens and parks*
> *sensitive to heat and aridity*

needles up to 1cm long

bluish-green, soft

Sitka Spruce
Picea sitchensis (pine family)
H 15–35 m May

Habitat *Native to the west coast of North America. In forests in north-west Europe and occasionally in parks. Distinctive light brown-coloured cones.*

> the largest species of Spruce, grows up to 85m in its natural habitat
> often weakened by air pollutants
> life span up to 800 years

The stable but light wood of the Sitka Spruce can be utilised in all kinds of ways. In the past, it played a key role in aircraft construction. Even Lindbergh's single-engined aeroplane 'Spirit of St. Louis', with which he became the first person to fly solo and non-stop across the Atlantic in 1927, was made mostly from this wood.

branches upswept, later horizontal

sharp tip

glossy green above

silvery white below

needles 1.5–2.5cm long

needles grow around the twig

crown broadly conical

cones hanging, up to 8cm long

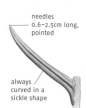

Japanese Cedar
Cryptomeria japonica (redwood family)
H 6–20m February–March

Habitat *Native to the mountains of Japan and China. In parks of central Europe. Un-mistakable owing to its characteristic needles.*

> needles often turn reddish-brown during frost
> needs sufficient humidity
> can live up to 500 years

The Japanese Cedar is the most important species of tree in Japan's forestry industry. Its non-resinous wood serves as a building material for a range of wooden constructions and bridges, and is also popularly used to manufacture barrels and vats. It is extremely long-lasting, even when it comes into contact with moisture.

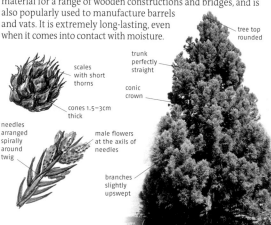

needles 0.6–2.5cm long, pointed

always curved in a sickle shape

scales with short thorns

cones 1.5–3cm thick

needles arranged spirally around twig

male flowers at the axils of needles

tree top rounded

trunk perfectly straight

conic crown

branches slightly upswept

Dawn Redwood

Metasequoia glyptostroboides (redwood family)
H 20–35m May

Shortly after the Second World War and not long after its discovery, the Dawn Redwood was planted as an attraction in many European parks. At first it was propogated solely using cuttings, which sprout roots easily. However, because of this, a large number of trees have the same genetic make-up and thus often have extremely similar forms. Nowadays these trees can be found in many countries around the world.

male flowers overhanging in clusters

crown sparse and conical

branches horizontal or slightly upswept

Habitat Only grows in the wild in one small area of China. Found in parks and gardens in Europe. Needles turn a distinctive orange to copper red in autumn.

> **needles and short side twigs drop in autumn**
> **considered to be a living fossil**
> **sensitive to late frosts**

opposite on short twigs

needles 1–3cm long, flat, light green

cones almost spherical, up to 2.5cm in size

blue-green when young

cones extremely woody when mature

usually has branches down to the ground

Did you know?

The first clue to this tree's existence was in fossils found in deposits from the Jurassic Period. In 1941, however, living trees were discovered in a small area of China – a sensation for botanists and palaeontologists alike!

Swamp Cypress

Taxodium distichum (redwood family)
H 20–35m March–April

Habitat *From swampy regions in the south-east of North America. Found in parks in Europe. Forms roots that rise out of ground in wet locations.*

> **needles drop along with short twigs in autumn**
> **sprouts from stumps**
> **can stand in water**

The significance of the strange roots, which rise out of the ground in many examples of the Swamp Cypress, has not yet been fully explained. It was once thought that these 'knee roots' were there to ensure sufficient supplies of oxygen for submerged parts in times of high water levels. Today it is believed that they help the trees to maintain their stability in soft swampy ground. Even strong storms rarely blow over Swamp Cypresses.

needles up to 2cm long, thin, flat, light green

alternate on short twigs

crown conical, broader in older trees

branches well spaced

cones spherical, up to 3cm in size

few scales

Did you know?
Along with the Dawn Redwood (p. 29) and larches (p. 44–45), the Swamp Cypress is one of the few conifers to shed its needles. Some plant lovers have misinterpreted the magnificent autumn colouring, believing the tree to be diseased.

Coast Redwood

Sequoia sempervirens (redwood family)
H 20–30m February–March

This mighty tree can live to between 1,000 and 1,500 years. For many Americans it is a symbol of durability. However, around 85 per cent of rainforests where the tree grew on the coast of California have been destroyed since it was first utilised. The durable wood is in great demand worldwide.

scales splayed out

crown slender and conical

branches in uneven whorls

branches strong, horizontal, often slightly hanging

cones up to 2.5cm long

Habitat Naturally occurring in western North America. In mild regions of Europe in gardens and parks, occasionally in forests.

> evergreen
> **can grow to more than 100m tall in its native habitat**
> **also known as the 'California Redwood'**

needles 0.6–2cm long, dark green, glossy

2 rows on short twigs

Prickly Juniper

Juniperus oxycedrus (juniper family)
H 2–15m February–March

In ancient times, juniper species growing as a tree were known as 'cedars'. The scientific species name *oxycedrus* means something like 'red cedar' and refers to the colour of the fruit. Sometimes the small tree or shrub is also called a Prickly Cedar, which can lead to confusion.

berry-like cones around 1cm thick

uneven crown

red-brown when mature

branches very dense, stiff

Habitat In shrub stands and open forests around the Mediterranean. Easily distinguished from Common Juniper (p. 32) by red-brown fruits.

> **also known as 'Cade Juniper'**
> **mostly on stony or sandy ground**
> fruits ripen twice a year

2 white central bands above

1.2–1.8cm long

3 projecting, rigid needles in a whorl

Common Juniper
Juniperus communis (juniper family)
H 2–10m April–May

Habitat *Heaths, rough pastures, open, dry forests from Europe to northern China. Fruits only turn blue and ripen in the second or third year.*

> not eaten by grazing animals
> has a strong, aromatic scent when crushed
> the typical tree or shrub of juniper heaths

In the past, people used to burn juniper twigs to fumigate homes and stables in times of human or animal epidemics. They believed that the powerful, bitter-tangy smoke could exorcise evil and all kinds of demons. The fruits also contain aromatic essential oils and are used to season sauerkraut and game. However, if eaten in excessive quantities they can irritate the kidneys. Gin, Genever and Germany's Steinhäger gin obtain their special flavour from the fruit distillates.

sharply pointed

1 white central band above

3 projecting needles in a whorl

1–2cm long

variable form, broad or pillar-shaped

often has multiple stems

berry-like cones blue-black, pruinose

pea-sized

Did you know?
The Dwarf Juniper (Juniperus communis ssp. alpina) is a subspecies of the Common Juniper. It grows in the Alps and other high mountains. In the Himalayas, it is found at altitudes of more than 3,500 metres – a record for a tree.

Japanese Plum Yew

Cephalotaxus harringtonia (plum-yew family)
H 3–10m April–May

Japanese Plum Yew trees are less hardy than Yews (p. 34) and are therefore grown far less often. They are sensitive to excessive sunshine. The seeds slightly resemble small plums. The seed coat is fleshy and resinous on the outside and hard and woody on the inside. An oil can be extracted from the stones and used as fuel.

Habitat *Native to Japan, China and Korea. Found in parks and gardens in Europe. The seeds are mostly single or in pairs.*

> similar to a long-needled **Yew** apart from fruit
> male and female trees
> also suitable as a hedge

in Europe, usually with multiple stems, shrub-like, occasionally tree-like with a broad crown

seeds up to 3cm long, oval

brown when ripe

needles up to 3.5cm long and 0.3cm wide

leathery, flexible, glossy

parted at the twig

Monkey Puzzle Tree

Araucaria araucana (monkey-puzzle family)
H 8–30m June–July

This unusual tree does not just attract attention in our gardens – it is considered to be one of the most impressive conifers of the southern hemisphere. In its native habitat, it is a protected species. The Pehuenche Indians who live in the Monkey Puzzle forests worship the tree as sacred, and eat its seeds, which are rich in fat and protein.

Habitat *Native to the Andes in Chile and Argentina. Found in parks and gardens in Europe. Unmistakable owing to the broad needles arranged in spirals.*

> only hardy in mild locations in Europe
> edible seeds
> male and female trees

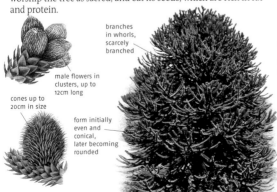

branches in whorls, scarcely branched

male flowers in clusters, up to 12cm long

cones up to 20cm in size

form initially even and conical, later becoming rounded

pointed

needles up to 5cm long

triangular, stiff

Yew

Taxus baccata (yew family)
H 2–15m March–April

Habitat *Rarely wild in European mountain forests. Often found in gardens, parks and cemeteries. Particularly distinctive because of its fruit.*

> grows as a tree or shrub
> extremely poisonous apart from red seed coat
> grows very slowly

In ancient times, the Yew was consecrated to the gods of the dead because of its extreme toxicity. But this long-lived tree was also a symbol of immortality and endurance. When cattle were still let loose to graze in woodlands, people felled many Yews because animals often died as a result of eating them. This and the intensive use of the wood have meant that there are now far fewer trees growing in the wild than in the past.

seeds surrounded by a red, fleshy seed coat

crown broadly conical, later rounded

2 broad, indistinct bands below

glossy dark green above

needles 2–3.5cm long, flexible, leathery

nut-like seeds

needles on horizontal twigs in 2 rows

male flowers spherical, up to 4mm in size

forms one or more trunks

Did you know?

Yew wood is heavy, hard and yet highly flexible. Even 'Özi', the Stone Age man found in an Alpine glacier, had a bow made of Yew with him. In the Middle Ages, people used Yew wood to make cross-bows and measuring tools and for woodturning work.

Mountain Pine

Pinus mugo (pine family)
H 2–4m June–July

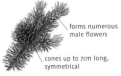

forms numerous male flowers

cones up to 7cm long, symmetrical

The Mountain Pine has highly flexible branches, which enable it to cope with the often heavy and long snow coverage in its natural habitat. The Mountain Pine oil obtained from the tree is a popular remedy. When inhaled, it can help soothe catarrh in the respiratory tracts and when rubbed on can ease muscle and joint pain.

Habitat *Mountains in central Europe. Grows as a 'krummholz' tree above the forest line in the Alps. In the first year the cones are green.*

forms multiple low-lying or climbing stems

mostly shrub-like

> *also known as the 'Mugo Pine'*
> *can grow in rock crevices*
> *frequently found as cultivars in gardens*

3–8cm long, slightly curved

dark green, rough needles in pairs

Mountain Pine ssp. *uncinata*

Pinus uncinata (pine family)
H 10–20m June–July

The Mountain Pine ssp. *uncinata* is closely related to the Mountain Pine although it has a completely different form, resembling the Scots Pine (p. 36). The trees play an important role in the mountains, stabilising scree and forming avalanche protection forests. However, there are also dwarf varieties that grow very compactly, almost in a cushion shape, and are suitable for rockeries.

Habitat *Western Alps, Pyrenees, Spain, upland moors in the Alpine foothills. Cones are always characteristically crooked and asymmetrical.*

bark grey-brown up to the crown area

erect tree with one or more trunks

> *needles like the Mountain Pine*
> *also known as 'Swiss Mountain Pine'*
> *grows right up to the tree line*

3–8cm long, slightly curved

dark green, rough needles in pairs

Scots Pine
Pinus sylvestris (pine family)
H 15–40m May–June

Habitat *Naturally occurring from Scotland to Mongolia and from Finland to the Mediterranean. Usually up to three cones next to each other.*

> **form differs depending on location**
> **largest distribution area of all pine species**
> **needs sufficient light**

The name 'pine' is derived from the Old English 'pin' and Latin 'pinus'. The resinous pinewood chips for burning were often the only source of lighting in the past. Spirits of turpentine and colophony were produced from the resin that flows out of fissured trunks. Cobbler's wax and tar were also made from it. The fossilised resin known as amber often originates from pine species.

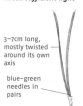

3–7cm long, mostly twisted around its own axis

blue-green needles in pairs

crown slender and conical to umbrella-shaped

bark red-brown to rust red, especially atop

36

abundant yellow male flowers

cones mostly crooked at base

cones 3–6cm long

trunk usually slender

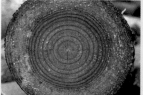

Did you know?
This tree is one of the most important timber species in Europe and Asia. Its wood is not only used for Scandinavian Pine furniture, but also makes excellent windows, doors and interiors.

European Black Pine

Pinus nigra (pine family)

H 20–30m May–June

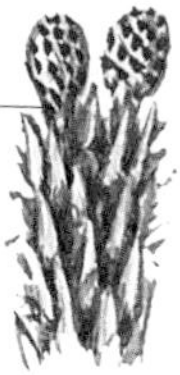

female flowers at ends of shoots

The cones open when the weather is dry and close again in damp weather conditions. This mechanism ensures that the winged seeds are only blown away by the wind when the flying conditions are good. The species tolerates salt water and is therefore suitable for planting near the coast. This name 'Black Pine' refers to the bark, which is often very dark.

Habitat *Naturally occurring from southern Europe to Austria and the Carpathians. In forests, gardens and parks to the north of these areas. Bark with deep fissures.*

> *various subspecies exist*
> *resilient in arid conditions*
> *stands up well to storms*

crown conical at first, later broadly spreading and rounded

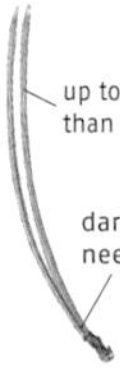

up to more than 10cm long

dark green needles in pairs

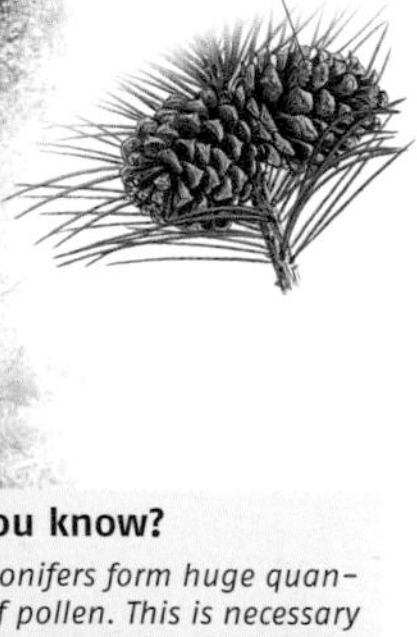

37

cones 3–8cm long, oval

Did you know?

Many conifers form huge quantities of pollen. This is necessary because the wind has to be able to blow the lightweight powder onto the female flowers. During the process, a lot goes astray. The 'sulphur rain' gathers in puddles and on cars – and triggers hay fever.

Aleppo Pine
Pinus halepensis (pine family)
H 10–20m March–May

Habitat *Native to the Mediterranean region. Solitary or in forests, often used for reforesting as well. Cones with a characteristically curved stem.*

> **cones remain on twig for several years**
> **needs plenty of light**
> **frequently affected by forest fires**

6–15cm long, pointed

less than 1mm thick

light green needles in pairs

The Aleppo Pine forms large quantities of resin. Its wood is thus excellent for pine chips, which people once burned for light when out fishing at night. The resin itself was for many years the cornerstone of a resin-processing industry in the Mediterranean area. Nowadays, only small quantities are collected and are mainly used to give Greek retsina wine its typical flavour.

trunk and branches mostly crooked

crown conical at first, later domed, like storeys of a building, slightly spherical

glossy

cones 5–12cm long, oval/conical

Did you know?
Caterpillars of the Eastern Pine Processionary Moth often eat pine trees in southern Europe. In their search for food, they walk behind one another in characteristic processions. They spend the night together in web-like nests, which can be spotted from afar.

Lodgepole Pine

Pinus contorta (pine family)
H 10–15m May–June

Forest fires, which frequently occur in America, assist the reproduction of the Lodgepole Pine. The cones, which hang on the trees for several years, open during great heat and release the seeds. These germinate particularly well when the ground is covered with fertile ash after fires.

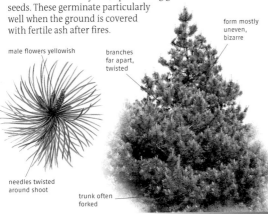

male flowers yellowish

needles twisted around shoot

branches far apart, twisted

form mostly uneven, bizarre

trunk often forked

Habitat Native to North America. Occasionally in gardens and parks in Europe and forests in Scotland. Usually several cones next to each other.

> *undemanding in natural habitat*
> *used to make paper in Canada and the United States*
> *also known as the 'Beach Pine'*

twisting around 360°

dark green needles in pairs

Maritime Pine

Pinus pinaster (pine family)
H 20–40m May

cones 10–20cm long

The Maritime Pine can grow even in sandy soils with few nutrients. This is why it is popular for reforesting dunes and other sandy areas. In central Europe, the tree is not hardy enough to survive the winters. In Germany, it is sometimes known as the 'Stern-Kiefer' or 'Star Pine', because the cones are often attached to the twig in the shape of a star.

Habitat Central and western Mediterranean region, Atlantic coast of Portugal and France. Cones very large, slightly asymmetrical

> *cones remain on tree for years*
> *longest pine needles in Europe*
> *used in forestry worldwide*

crown more or less oval, often uneven

needles relatively sparse

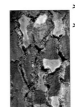

bark with red-brown scales

stiff, pointed

10–25cm long, 2mm wide

glossy, dark green needles in clusters of 2

Stone Pine
Pinus pinea (pine family)
H 15–30m April–May

The flat crown has two advantages for the Stone Pine: it provides shade on the ground, thus protecting the roots from drying out too much. It also only offers little resistance to the frequently strong coastal winds. The kernels have a pleasant, almond-like taste. However, the generally very hard seed coats have to be cracked to reach them.

glossy brown

cones up to 14cm long and 10cm thick

crown distinctively umbrella-shaped, flat domed, spherical on young trees

sharp tip

up to 15cm long, stiff

dark green needles in pairs

seeds with woody coat

bark deeply fissured

Did you know?
Pine nuts were evidently used by the ancient Romans to feed their troops while on the march. In England, seed coats were found in the refuse pits of Roman camps.

Ponderosa Pine

Pinus ponderosa (pine family)

H 15–50m May–June

cones up to 15cm long

oval

The Ponderosa Pine – or Western Yellow Pine – got its name from the yellowish wood, which is very heavy. Since the trees grow very straight and form strong trunks, they are among the most economically important wood suppliers in North America. Pine trees, particularly the Ponderosa Pine, react sensitively to ozone levels in the air.

straight trunk, right up to tree top

crown slender and conical

branches far apart

inconspicuous female flowers

male flowers up to 3.5cm long, yellow or red

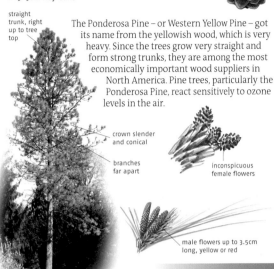

Habitat Naturally occurring in western North America up to altitudes of 2,700m. Grows in parks in Europe. Twigs often strongly backward-curving.

> can live to 500 years
> is very common in its natural habitat
> highly furrowed, thick bark

12–25cm long

dark green needles in clusters of 3

Eastern White Pine

Pinus strobus (pine family)

H 20–50m May–June

The Eastern White Pine produces large quantities of wood. It is one of the highest yielding conifers in its native habitat and is sometimes referred to as the 'King's Pine'. The masts of large sailing ships were often made of the straight, highly resilient trunks of this species; even buildings were made from it.

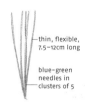

Habitat Native to the eastern United States and Canada. In forests and parks in Europe. Young cones standing on ends of twigs.

> supplies lightweight, very soft wood
> also known as 'Weymouth Pine' or 'Northern White Pine'
> hardy in winter

crown sparse and conical, broader in older trees

usually slightly bent

branches projecting almost at right angles from trunk

cones up to 20cm long, cylindrical

thin, flexible, 7.5–12cm long

blue-green needles in clusters of 5

Swiss Pine

Pinus cembra (pine family)
H 10–20m June

Habitat In central Europe in the Alps and Carpathians, in the flatlands of northern Siberia. Young cones are violet.

> also known as the 'Arolla Pine'
> supplies excellent wood for wood sculptors
> popular in gardens

Pine nuts can sometimes be bought as a snack or to go in muesli. These are actually the kernels of a subspecies of the Swiss Pine, which grows in Siberia's taiga (boreal forest). The cones do not open on the tree, but drop whole. The seeds are then usually devoured by rodents and birds, which find them tasty and nutritious.

violet at first, then cinnamon-brown

cones oval, 6–8cm long

crown conical at first, later broadly rounded, often uneven

dark green needles in clusters of 5

fairly stiff, 5–8cm long

dense branches and twigs

Did you know?

Swiss Pines tolerate extreme cold and grow right up to the tree line. One of the most beautiful Swiss Pine forests in the Alps lies in the UNESCO world natural heritage site of Aletsch in Switzerland. The European Larch (p. 44) also grows there at lower altitudes.

Japanese White Pine

Pinus parviflora (pine family)
H 3–8m May–June

In Japan, the Japanese White Pine not only grows in the wild – it is also frequently cultivated. There is hardly a Japanese garden without one or more examples of this species. Low, compact forms with shorter needles, which are grown as Bonsai trees, are especially popular there. Different varieties are also grown in Europe.

Habitat *Native to Japan. Found in parks and gardens in Europe. Cones remain on the tree for several years.*

> **can grow up to 30m tall in Japan**
> **thrives in damp soils**
> **trees often cultivated with 'step-like' branches**

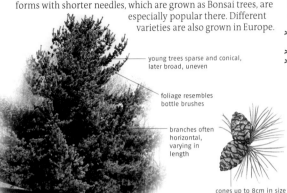

young trees sparse and conical, later broad, uneven

foliage resembles bottle brushes

branches often horizontal, varying in length

cones up to 8cm in size

blue-green needles in clusters of 5

twisted and bent, 4–7cm long

Blue Pine

Pinus wallichiana (pine family)
H 15–30m May–June

The Blue Pine produces large, glossy droplets of resin, which hang like tears especially on young cones. The tree sometimes forms dense forests in the Himalayas. In Afghanistan, it grows at altitudes of up to 4,000 metres. In central Europe, it decorates many gardens and parks with its elegant appearance.

Habitat *Naturally occurring from the Himalayas to Afghanistan. As single trees in gardens and parks in Europe. Needles droop from the twigs.*

> **not tolerant of too much sun in winter**
> **sensitive to frosts when young**
> **elegant ornamental tree**

branches far apart

form broadly conical

cones may be more than 25cm long, hanging

up to 20cm long, thin, drooping

usually curving form

green needles in clusters of 5

European Larch

Larix decidua (pine family)
H 25–35m April–May

male flowers
yellowish

female flowers red-violet

Habitat *Originally grew wild in the Alps and Carpathians. Widespread in forests, parks and gardens. Trees glow golden-yellow in autumn.*

This is Europe's only native conifer to lose its foliage in autumn. Larch wood is very long-lasting and resistant to fungi, leaching, acids and water. It was used to make water pipes for many hundreds of years. Nowadays it is used as building wood for windows and doors, as well as for interior work and furniture because of its beautiful grain.

> grows up to the tree line in high mountains
> needs plenty of light
> can live up to 600 years

cones up to 4cm long, brown

clinging scales

even, conical crown

light green to dark green needles in clusters of 30–40

branches almost horizontal to overhanging

up to 3cm long

thin twigs, hanging from main branches

twigs bare in winter with protuberances

Did you know?

Larch resin always remains liquid, unlike pine resin which solidifies when dry. It was once known as 'Venetian turpentine' and used to treat rheumatism and other complaints. Pitch made from the resin was used to waterproof beer barrels.

Japanese Larch

Larix kaempferi (pine family)
H 25–30m April–May

female flowers
mainly yellow-
green

The Japanese Larch needs plenty of water and therefore reaches for it with its roots deep down into the earth. In wet coastal areas of Europe, it is now grown more frequently than the European Larch (p. 44). Its wood is similar to that of the European species and is also used for interior work.

crown conical, broad in older trees

Habitat *Originated in Japan. Found in forests, gardens and parks in Europe. Needles turn golden-yellow in autumn.*

> *grows faster than the European Larch*
> *empty cones remain on the tree for years*
> *sensitive to late frosts*

cones up to 3.5cm long

branches project horizontally, strong

edge of scales bent over

male flowers yellow

bluish-green needles in clusters of 20–40

up to 3.5cm long

45

Deodar

Cedrus deodara (pine family)
H 20–25m September

leading shoots long, generally overhanging

Out of the three species of cedar described in this book, the Deodar is the most sensitive. Although it grows at altitudes of up to 3,000 metres in its natural habitat, the tough central European winters often damage it so much that it loses its beautiful form. Numerous magnificent examples of all three species can be found in southern Europe.

Habitat *Native to the Himalayas. In areas of Europe with mild winters, it makes a beautiful tree in parks and gardens. All cedars flower in autumn.*

> *needs sufficient humidity*
> *also known as the 'Himalayan Cedar'*
> *grown as a weeping tree in gardens*

branches horizontal with hanging tips

conical crown

up to 6.5cm long, soft, evergreen

dark green needles in clusters of 25–30

cones up to 12cm long

Atlas Cedar

Cedrus atlantica (pine family)
H 10–20m September

cones cylindrical,
up to 8cm long

Habitat Originated in the Atlas Mountains of north Africa. Frequently in parks and gardens in Europe. Often forms cones on lower twigs.

> life span up to 900 years
> also known as the 'Atlantic Cedar'
> most widely spread cedar species in our gardens

Cedar oil can be obtained from the wood of cedars. The ancient Egyptians believed that its aroma could aid reincarnation and thus embalmed their dead with it. These days, a slightly volatile cedar oil, which is extracted from the wood or needles by a special process, is used in aromatherapy. Burning just a few drops in an oil burner releases a woody, balsamic scent, which imparts a feeling of strength and self-confidence.

needles up to 3cm long, relatively stiff

mostly blue-green needles in clusters of 10–40

leading shoot erect or slightly slanting at most

tree top flat

male flowers up to 5cm long

on upper side of twigs

46

form remains conical even on old trees

Did you know?

The name 'Cedar' is only used to describe the aromatic wood of a true species of cedar in rare cases. The word 'cedar' is more often used to describe other, unrelated aromatic woods than it is to describe true species of cedar. The term is more commonly used for species such as the Virginian Juniper (p. 56) or Western Red Cedar (p. 55).

Lebanon Cedar
Cedrus libani (pine family)
H 20–35m September

This impressive cedar was once believed to be the most beautiful tree. The last survivors of the forests on Mount Lebanon are still known as the 'Cedars of God' today. The wood has been used intensively for some 5,000 years. In ancient Egypt, Greece and Phoenicia, it was used in the building of magnificent temples and ships. However, the former mighty forests have shrunk drastically after centuries of deforestation.

crown broad, umbrella–shaped on older trees

generally with multiple very strong branches projecting steeply upwards

Habitat *Native to Asia Minor and west Asia. In parks and gardens, particularly in western Europe. Scales of mature cones drop.*

> **mentioned as far back as the Old Testament**
> **cones slightly larger than those of the Atlas Cedar**
> **highly attractive park tree in areas with mild winters**

needles up to 3.5cm long, pointed

light to dark green needles in clusters of 10–20

47

Japanese Umbrella Pine
Sciadopitys verticillata (redwood family)
H 10–30m May

male flowers on tips of twigs

This tree is special because its needles differ from those of other conifers. Botanists are not sure whether the leaves consist of two needles that have fused together or a modified shoot. In Japan, the Japanese Umbrella Pine is frequently cultivated in temple grounds and gardens. Illustrations of the characteristic twigs are used to decorate porcelain, room dividers and lacquered goods. The tree is grown for the forestry industry, supplying white, flexible timber for ships and buildings.

Habitat *Native to Japan. Occasionally in parks and gardens in central Europe. Distinctive needles resembling umbrella spokes.*

> **often only grows as a shrub in Europe**
> **cones ripen in the second year**
> **needs non-chalky soils**

form slender and conical, often uneven

generally resembles a small pine tree

cones woody, up to 10cm long

needles in whorls of 30–40

5–15cm long, leathery, flexible

Giant Sequoia
Sequoiadendron giganteum (redwood family)
H 30–100m May

This giant of a tree has inspired botanists to name it after different personalities: Wellingtonia comes from Sir Arthur Wellesley, Duke of Wellington, while President George Washington was honoured in the name *Sequoia washingtonia*, as was Native American Indian Sequoyah (1770–1843). The son of a Cherokee and a white fur trader, Sequoyah developed the first Native American alphabet and thus introduced writing to his people.

Habitat Native to the Sierra Nevada in North America. In parks and gardens and occasionally forests in central Europe. Bark sponge-like, soft.

> young trees grow extremely quickly
> cones ripen in the second year
> can live more than 3,000 years

needles cover twigs like scales

0.3–0.8cm long

pointed tip

young crown densely conical, later broad and unevenly rounded

Did you know?
There are 200,000 of the tiny seeds in every kilo. This was obviously a surprise to the person in the German region of Württemberg who ordered half a pound of them in 1864. Because of this, a fair number of large examples of around the same age can be found in Germany today particularly in the state of Baden-Württemberg.

cones oval, 5–8cm long

inconspicuous flowers

trunk broad at base

California Incense Cedar

Calocedrus decurrens (juniper family)
H 10–30m April–May

Native Americans once used the bark of the
California Incense Cedar to build huts.
The first white settlers also valued
the long strips, which they used for
roofing. The wood does not splinter
and can be sharpened easily, which is
why it has also been used to make
pencils for several decades.

form conical or
column-shaped

Habitat *Naturally
occurring in western
North America. In parks
in Europe. Cinnamon-
coloured bark detaches
in thin, scale-like
strips.*

> *also known as 'White
Cedar'*
> *twigs have an aromatic
scent when crushed*
> *life span up to 1,000
years*

2 scales split apart
when mature

cones
2–4cm long

branches
upwardly curved

trunk often
broad at base

scalated leaves
slender, glossy

tip does not
lie flat on
twig

Arizona Cypress

Cupressus arizonica (juniper family)
H 10–25m February–April

In southern Europe, the Arizona Cypress
is often planted in windbreak hedges
or to prevent soil erosion. The tree
can be recognised from afar due
to its grey-blue colour. During
the flowering season in spring,
it appears yellowish since
almost all of the twigs are
covered in an abundance
of small, yellow flowers.
The pollen is a well-known
trigger of hay fever.

branches
projecting
almost
horizontally

Habitat *Naturally
occurring from Arizona
to California and
Mexico, up to more
than 2,000m. In parks
and gardens in Europe.
Cones green at first,
later grey.*

> *very undemanding and
fairly hardy*
> *twigs have a pleasant
scent when crushed*
> *also available in a yellow
variety*

mature cones around
2.5cm in size

form conical
or oval

scales with
pointed
protuberance

spherical

scalated leaves
0.2–0.5cm
long, grey to
blue-green

dense
covering on
round shoots

Mediterranean Cypress

Cupressus sempervirens (juniper family)

H 20–30m March–May

scalated leaves dark green, form a dense covering like roof tiles

0.5–1mm in size, blunt

50

The column-shaped variety of the Mediterranean Cypress, which was planted widely by the Romans, remains an emblem of the Mediterranean region today. The wild form with more horizontal branches grows in forests. In ancient times, it apparently formed extensive forests on Crete and Cyprus. Because the trees supply highly durable wood, however, the cypresses were felled in large quantities to make ships, doors, coffins and other goods.

single cones

2.5–4cm when ripe

twigs thin, appear rectangular

dark green the whole year

wild form oval, otherwise mostly column-shaped with upswept branches

Did you know?

Cypresses were a symbol of mourning back in ancient Greece, whereas Christians see the evergreen cypress more as a tree of life. Both beliefs have led to column-shaped cypresses being a common sight in Mediterranean cemeteries.

Lawson's Cypress

Chamaecyparis lawsoniana (juniper family)

H 2–35m April

The wood has similar properties to that of the next species so it is not surprising that the Japanese like importing it from North America. From around 1920 until after the Second World War, the wood was even used to make battery separators.

tree top overhanging

crown slender and conical to cylindrical

branches horizontal, mostly hanging at the ends

Habitat *Native to North America. Frequently found as a cultivar in parks, gardens and cemeteries in Europe. Abundant red male flowers in spring.*

> *also grows in shady spots*
> *fruits ripen in the first year*
> *crushed twigs give off an aromatic scent*

scalated leaves slightly pointed

cones blue–white, pruinose initially

red-brown, woody, 0.8–1cm in size when ripe

male flowers up to 5mm long, red

indistinct white lines below

Hinoki Cypress

Chamaecyparis obtusa (juniper family)

H 0.5–15m April–May

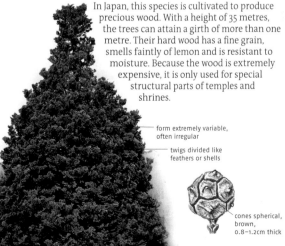

In Japan, this species is cultivated to produce precious wood. With a height of 35 metres, the trees can attain a girth of more than one metre. Their hard wood has a fine grain, smells faintly of lemon and is resistant to moisture. Because the wood is extremely expensive, it is only used for special structural parts of temples and shrines.

Habitat *Wild form in Japan. Mostly as smaller varieties in gardens and parks in Europe. Twigs often characteristically shell-shaped.*

> *also popular as a Bonsai tree*
> *numerous cultivars*
> *one of the most popular varieties is 'Fernspray Gold'*

form extremely variable, often irregular

twigs divided like feathers or shells

scalated leaves with blunt tips

cones spherical, brown, 0.8–1.2cm thick

dense covering on twig like roof tiles

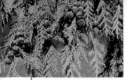

Nootka Cypress
Chamaecyparis nootkatensis (juniper family)

H 3–30m April–May

Habitat *Wild in north-west North America as far as southern Alaska. In parks and gardens in Europe. Distinctive hanging twigs, often with many cones.*

> **twigs smell of turpentine when crushed**
> **extremely hardy**
> **available in different varieties from nurseries**

This tree grows fairly slowly in its natural habitat and supplies firm, evenly structured wood. This is resistant to rot, even when outdoors or in a damp climate. Also known as 'Yellow Cedar' or 'Alaska Cedar', it is highly sought after as a building material for furniture, boats, shingles and veneer. The trees are therefore collected even from barely accessible locations by helicopter.

scalated leaves 0.3–0.6cm long with pronounced tips

projecting outwards at tip on strong twigs

unripe cones blue-green, pruinose

mature cones red-brown, around 1cm in size

scales with large protuberance

male flowers at ends of twigs

even, conical crown

branches dense, spreading, overhanging at ends

Did you know?
The popular garden variety 'Pendula' has branches that form arches from which the twigs droop down, giving the variety its other name: 'Weeping Nootka Falsecypress'.

Sawara Cypress
Chamaecyparis pisifera (juniper family)
H 0.5–20m April–May

crown extremely variable, often slender and conical

As with the other 'false' cypresses, numerous cultivars of this species can be found in gardens. These are often difficult to assign to a standard species. Many of the mutations do not produce cones. In Japan, the Sawara Cypress is one of the species cultivated to form the bizarre Bonsai trees.

Habitat *Wild form native to Japan. In gardens, parks and cemeteries in Europe. Cones remain on the tree all winter.*

> *life span up to 400 years*
> *many varieties in gardens*
> *some varieties form almost thread-like twigs*

twigs divided like feathers

10–12 scales with protuberances

pea-sized cones

white patches below

scalated leaves on edges slender with free-standing tips

53

Hiba
Thujopsis dolabrata (juniper family)
H 5–10m May

Although the tree has a similar form to the other Arborvitae species, a glance at the underside of the twigs is enough to identify it clearly since the distinctive white pattern is unmistakable. Scented Hiba wood oil is distilled from wood shavings and used as a natural fungicide. Oil extracts are also used to scent soaps.

Habitat *Native to the mountains of Japan. In parks and larger gardens in Europe. Undersides of twigs have a chalky appearance.*

> *grows extremely slowly, often just as a shrub*
> *needs damp soils*
> *branches at ground level can form roots*

form broadly conical, often with multiple stems

branches horizontal or upswept

cones up to 1.5cm long

scales with folded-back appendage

usually has branches down to the ground

scalated leaves up to 0.8cm long, leathery

white with just a narrow green edge below

Northern White Cedar

Thuja occidentalis (juniper family)
H 5–20m April–May

Habitat *Native to eastern North America. In parks, gardens and green areas in Europe. Cones standing on upper side of flat twigs.*

> **crushed twigs have a bitter and tangy scent**
> **damages the kidneys if consumed**
> **numerous cultivars**

The Northern White Cedar was brought to Europe from North America around 1536, making it one of the first trees to be imported from the New World. It is now one of our most popular garden trees. Extracts are used by doctors to treat certain skin diseases and warts. In the past, preparations were also wrongly taken to induce abortions – a treatment that could be fatal to the pregnant women.

cones oval, up to 1cm long

twigs spread out flat

'empty' cones often persist on twigs for a long time

inconspicuous flowers

scalated leaves blunt, up to 0.7cm long

distinctive resin gland

crown slender and conical

dense branches

Did you know?

Slender, column-shaped cultivars do not just add a special touch to gardens – in central Europe, they are popularly planted in cemeteries as well. There, they take on the role of the Mediterranean Cypress (p. 50) and are seen as a symbol of immortality.

branches reach a long way down

Western Red Cedar

Thuja plicata (juniper family)
H 15–30m May

This species is also known as the 'Giant Arborvitae'. It produces one of the lightest conifer woods, which is particularly good for making shingles. Since it also contains substances that prevent insect infestations and decay, it is popularly used to make posts, masts, log cabins, exterior cladding and saunas.

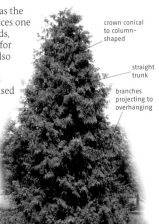

crown conical to column-shaped

straight trunk

branches projecting to overhanging

Habitat Native to western North America. In parks and occasionally forests in Europe. Upper and undersides of twigs differ considerably.

> **twigs have a pineapple aroma when crushed**
> **poisonous!**
> **life span up to 1,000 years**

woody scales with small thorn

cones around 1.2cm long

scalated leaves shiny green above

characteristic whitish pattern below

Chinese Arborvitae

Platycladus orientalis (juniper family)
H 5–10m April–May

crown conical or rounded

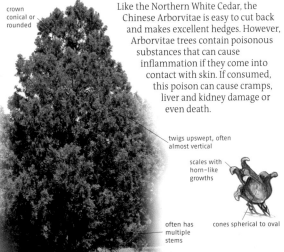

Like the Northern White Cedar, the Chinese Arborvitae is easy to cut back and makes excellent hedges. However, Arborvitae trees contain poisonous substances that can cause inflammation if they come into contact with skin. If consumed, this poison can cause cramps, liver and kidney damage or even death.

Habitat Native to east Asia where it has been cultivated for many years. In gardens, parks and cemeteries in Europe. Unripe cones a distinctive blue–green colour.

> **crushed twigs have a slightly resinous scent**
> **poisonous!**
> **often brownish in winter**

twigs upswept, often almost vertical

scales with horn-like growths

often has multiple stems

cones spherical to oval

scalated leaves bright green to yellow-green

both sides the same colours

Virginian Juniper
Juniperus virginiana (juniper family)
H 2–18m March–May

Habitat *Wild form in North America. In Europe, mostly as a cultivar in parks and gardens. Blue, pruinose berry-like cones mature in first year.*

> *intensive, tangy scent*
> *largest species of Juniper, trunk up to 30m tall in its native habitat*
> *many varieties known*

Also known as the 'Eastern Red Cedar', this tree supplied the classic wood for pencils for many years. The wood has a uniform structure and can be worked easily. With these properties, the tree should be of interest to the European forestry industry. However, attempts by Prussian foresters to grow it did not meet with the desired success since the trees grew too slowly in our climate. Various ornamental forms have become popular garden trees.

sharp needles and scalated leaves on the same tree

scalated leaves up to 3.5mm long, grey-green

tree top mostly rounded

crown broadly conical, also column-shaped in cultivars

berry-like cones blue, pruinose, 0.3–0.7cm thick

Did you know?
The central woody part of the trunk has a characteristic red-violet colour when freshly sawn. Pieces of the wood make an effective moth deterrent when placed in cupboards as insects avoid the aromatic scent.

Ginkgo

Ginkgo biloba (ginkgo family)
H 10–40m April

Ancestors of the Ginkgo, which were very similar to today's species, populated the Earth back in the Jurassic Period. The Ginkgo is the sole survivor of this group, making it a living fossil. It is so robust that it copes well with air pollution in city centres. One Ginkgo tree even survived the atom bomb attack on Hiroshima and the tree has been a symbol of hope for the Japanese ever since.

Habitat *Wild in the Chinese province of Zhejiang only. In parks and streets in Europe. Characteristic leaves unmistakable.*

> *resembles a deciduous tree, but is actually related to the conifers*
> *male and female trees*
> *hardy*

inconspicuous female
flowers in clusters of 2–3

male flowers
in catkins

crown extremely
variable, often
broadly conical

leaf fan-shaped,
5–8cm wide,
leathery

leaf veins
forked

often notched at tip

57

generally few, but
strong branches

foliage golden
yellow in autumn

seeds plum-like,
2–3cm in size

Did you know?

The Chinese word 'Gin-kyo' means 'silver apricot' and refers to the appearance of the seeds. Their soft outer shells smell unpleasantly of sweaty feet. The hard inner shells surround a kernel, which the Japanese and Chinese roast and eat like pistachio nuts.

She-oak
Casuarina equisetifolia (beefwood family)
H 10–20m January–March

pine-like form

Habitat *Native to south-east Asia, Australia, Polynesia. Frequently planted in southern Europe. Extremely slender, needle-like twigs.*

> *tolerates salt*
> *even grows in pure sand*
> *also known as an 'Ironwood' or 'Australian Pine'*

Although the twigs resemble the branchlets of Equisetum or horsetails, the trees are not actually related at all. The She-oak stabilises dunes, acts as a windbreak and grows well in parks and streets in unfavourable, dry locations. The hard, red-brown wood makes durable shingles.

shoots thin, angular

tiny leaves at nodes

woody

crown slender, sparse, 'transparent'

straight trunk

cone-like fruits up to 2.5cm in size

58

Tree Heath
Erica arborea (heath family)
H 1–15m March–May

Habitat *Wild around the Mediterranean, on the Canary Islands and in the mountains of central Africa. Generally forms abundant flowers.*

> *flowers attract bees*
> *needle-like foliage adapted to aridity*
> *larger trees, particularly on the Canary Islands*

In French, the Tree Heath is known as 'bruyère', a name that has become widely used for the red-brown-grained root wood in other languages as well. The wood burns poorly so is mainly used to make pipe bowls. It also makes beautiful veneers.

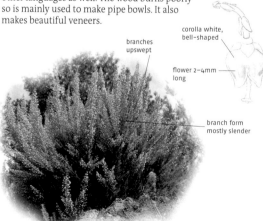

corolla white, bell-shaped

branches upswept

flower 2–4mm long

branch form mostly slender

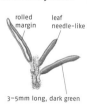

rolled margin

leaf needle-like

3–5mm long, dark green

Small-flowered Tamarisk

Tamarix parviflora (tamarisk family)
H 3–4m April–May

In ancient times, the tamarisk was a symbol of youth and beauty. According to Egyptian legend, the god Osiris was murdered and sealed in a chest, which was thrown into the Nile. The chest landed in the branches of a tamarisk tree, which grew to enclose it and became famous throughout the country. Today, the tamarisk is often found as an undemanding hedge plant in Greece.

Habitat *Originally occurring in the eastern Mediterranean. Now cultivated in southern and central Europe. Flowers before foliation.*

> tolerates a large amount of salt in the soil
> pioneer plant on shores and dunes
> popular ornamental tree in streets, parks and gardens

countless short flowering twigs

flower with 4 pink petals

twigs overhanging

one or more stems

leaves up to 4mm long, scale-shaped

leaves lie along branches

Salt Cedar

Tamarix ramosissima (tamarisk family)
H 3–5m July–September

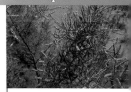

Tamarisks can grow in salt deserts. Although they take up salt in the groundwater, they can excrete it again through special glands on the leaves so that it does not harm them. They are therefore suitable for stabilising the ground or as ornamental trees near the coast within range of the salt spray.

Habitat *Native to the Caspian Sea coastline. Cultivated in southern and central Europe. Flowers have a slightly feathery appearance.*

> thrives on warmth and sunshine
> can be cut back extensively
> pale yellow in autumn

form sparse, broom-like

flower with 5 pale pink petals

branches generally upswept

mostly multiple stems

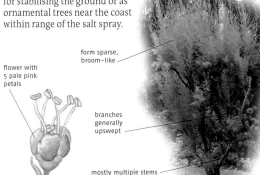

leaves scale-shaped, grey-green

leaves attached along twig

Common Beech
Fagus sylvatica (beech family)
H 25–30m April–May

Habitat Native to forests throughout most of Europe. Frequently cultivated in forests and parks. Closed fruits can be spotted by their spines.

> important supplier of wood
> sensitive to waterlogging
> highly tolerant of shade

If man did not interfere with nature, the Common Beech would be the most widepread species of tree in central Europe. Beech seeds (beechmast) were gathered as far back as pre-historic times. In times of need, they served as food right into the 20th century, being used for oil and flour. However, just a few seeds can cause vomiting and diarrhoea in some people. In the past, farmers let their pigs loose in the woods to forage for the fruits.

Bark grey, relatively smooth

leaf 5–15cm long, elliptic to oval

margin slightly wavy

pyramidal fruits known as 'beechmast'

woody fruit cup

female flowers erect

male flowers in hanging heads

crown often high-domed

broad or narrower depending on location

straight trunk, reaching far up into the crown

Did you know?
In storms, it is safer to shelter under beech trees than oaks. Lightning usually strikes high points such as single trees or towers. Since the Common Beech hardly ever stands alone, unlike oaks, it is struck more rarely. However, standing under tall trees is never advisable during a thunder storm!

Copper Beech

Fagus sylvatica 'purpurea' (beech family)
H 25–30m April–May

The Copper Beech is a mutation of the Common Beech, differing only in colour. From the sixth century, Common Beech wood was used to make writing tablets, several of which were then bound together, giving rise to the word 'book' from the Anglo Saxon 'boc', meaning 'beech'.

Habitat *Ornamental garden form so only in gardens and parks. Unmistakable due to leaf colour.*

> *red colouring covers green of the leaves*
> *very dark in appearance*
> *also popular in gardens as a weeping tree*

Crown convex, rounded

branches with many twigs

branches steeply ascending

leaf 5–18cm long, elliptic to oval

margin slightly wavy

dark red to almost black

61

Holm Oak

Quercus ilex (beech family)
H 5–25m April–May

The bark of the Holm Oak contains large quantities of tanning agents and is used to tan leather. The wood makes excellent charcoal. A sweet-fruiting variety of Holm Oak is grown in Spain and North Africa. The fruits of this form (*Quercus ilex ballota*) can be roasted or eaten raw.

Habitat *Native to forests and copses in the Mediterranean. In parks in England. Distinctive due to firm, dark green leaves.*

> *evergreen*
> *hardy in Britain*
> *leaf shape extremely variable*

numerous strong branches

rounded crown

leaf margin also toothed

grey, felted below

acorn up to 3cm long

half enclosed in fruit cup

trunk generally short

leaf shiny dark green above

pointed

2–8cm long, leathery

Osier
Salix viminalis (willow family)
H 2–10m March–April

Habitat *Wild from Europe to Siberia in water meadows and on banks of streams, often planted for weaving purposes. Twigs extremely flexible.*

> cut trees known as 'pollarded willows'
> can sometimes stand in water
> also known as the 'Basket Willow'

leaf up to 20cm long, slender and lanceolate

margin rolled downwards

densely covered in silky hairs below

Radically pruned Osiers form a mass of long, branchless rods – classic raw material for basket weavers. For large baskets, weavers leave the rods as they are, whereas for more delicate baskets, they generally remove the bark so that the light wood can be seen. The rods are soaked in water until they become soft and flexible and can be woven well. The basketwork becomes firm as it dries.

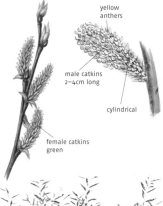

yellow anthers

male catkins 2–4cm long

cylindrical

female catkins green

Did you know?
Other species of osier also supply weaving materials – often with differently coloured barks. Basket weavers also create colour variants by boiling or staining the rods.

twigs mostly thick at base

long, straight twigs

trunk often crooked or with multiple stems

Osage-orange

Maclura pomifera (mulberry family)
H 10–15m May–June

hard thorns, up to 3cm long, on twigs

This tree was named after the Osage Indians who lived in Oklahoma and carved their bows from the hard wood. The fruit cannot be eaten by humans – even animals barely touch it. Scientists surmise that it was once eaten by large mammals, such as Columbian mammoths and mastodons, which are now extinct.

green in summer

crown sparse, often irregular

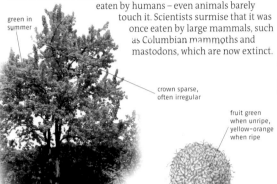

Habitat *Native to North America. Partially naturalised in southern Europe, in parks of central Europe. Fruits resemble unripe oranges.*

> *damaged leaves produce a milky sap*
> *male and female trees*
> *also grown as hedges in southern Europe*

fruit green when unripe, yellow-orange when ripe

wrinkled

8–12cm thick, hard

leaf oval, 5–12cm long

shiny above

pointed

Persian Ironwood

Parrotia persica (witch-hazel family)
H 5–10m March

capsule fruits open with 2–4 flaps

In its natural habitat, the Persian Ironwood can form forests that are reminiscent of beech forests. Its wood has been used intensively for centuries. The tree is known as the 'Ironwood' because its wood is extremely hard and heavier than water. The tree was named *Parrotia* in honour of the German doctor and botanist F. W. Parrot, who was the first European to climb Mount Ararat in the native habitat of the Persian Ironwood in 1829.

Habitat *Native to northern Iran and the Caucasus. In parks and gardens in Europe. Foliage bright yellow and red for a long period in autumn.*

> *leaves similar to those of the Common Beech (p. 60)*
> *bark peels off in large scales*
> *flowers before foliation*

crown broad and domed, often broader than it is high

form variable with one or more, often crooked stems

stamens red

flowers in heads

leaf 6–10cm long, lopsided, oval

blunt tip

margin wavy, occasionally crenate

Southern Magnolia
Magnolia grandiflora (magnolia family)
H 5–30m May–August

dark foliage often makes for a gloomy appearance

crown slender and high

Habitat *Native to southern North America, frequently found in southern Europe, occasionally planted in mild areas of central Europe. Flowers up to 20cm wide.*

> *also known as the 'Bull Bay'*
> *barely hardy in Britain*
> *foliage resembles that of a rubber plant*

The phylogeny of the magnolia family goes back 150 million years, making them among the most ancient seed plants. The Southern Magnolia is considered to be one of the oldest of the magnolias owing to its persistent leaves.

fruit upright, cone-like

glossy dark green above

brownish hairs below

leaf 12–20cm long

64

Kobus Magnolia
Magnolia kobus (magnolia family)
H 8–10m April–May

Habitat *Native to Japan. In parks and gardens in mild areas of Europe. Abundant white flowers appear before leaves.*

> *flowers scented*
> *needs damp soils*
> *particularly attractive as a single tree*

crown broadly rounded or conical

The Kobus Magnolia takes a few years to flower regularly after planting, but the magnificent flowers are worth waiting for. Magnolias were named after the French doctor and botanist, Pierre Magnol, who lived from 1638 to 1715. He was the first to introduce the term 'family' to classify plants into larger groups of related species.

margin wavy

lighter below

leaf 6–12cm long, lopsided, oval

pointed tip

flower around 10cm wide

6–9 petals

trunk generally short

Saucer Magnolia

Magnolia x *soulangiana* (magnolia family)

H 3–6m April–May

The first Saucer Magnolia was created around 1820 on an estate near Paris as a random hybrid of two species from China: the Mulan Magnolia and Yulan Magnolia. Nowadays there are many varieties on the market. Occasionally, the trees form a few flowers in summer as well in spring. The tree is sometimes incorrectly referred to as a 'Tulip Tree' (p. 127).

Habitat *Frequently found in gardens and parks in areas of Europe that are not too cold, does not grow wild. Abundant flowers before foliation.*

> magnificent garden tree
> attracts beetles as pollinators
> needs a protected location

cone-like fruit

flowers up to 30cm wide

8–10 white or pink petals

pointed

matt dark green

leaf 10–18cm long, lopsided, oval

broad crown

65

lower branches broadly spreading

often has branches near the ground

Did you know?

As long as the buds are surrounded by their hairy scales, they cannot be damaged by frost. However, if they get caught by a cold spell later, the flowers will not appear.

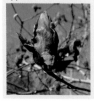

Avocado

Persea americana (bay family)
H 5–15m   March–April

Habitat *Originally from Mexico, Central America and Columbia. Cultivated in the Mediterranean. Forms only a few fruits despite producing many flowers.*

> **many cultivated varieties found in warm areas worldwide**
> **also known as an 'Alligator Pear'**
> **only one in every 5,000 flowers produces a fruit**

The nutritious fruits were enjoyed by America's native inhabitants. In Columbia, archaeologists found the remains of avocados in settlements that were around 10,000 years old. The buttery, easily digestible fruit flesh contains between four and 30 per cent fat, depending on the variety, as well as minerals, vitamins, protein and some carbohydrates.

crown rounded to hemispherical

flower yellow-green

6 petals

evergreen

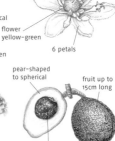

pear-shaped to spherical

fruit up to 15cm long

leaf up to 20cm long, elliptic

evergreen

one large seed

Bay Laurel

Laurus nobilis (bay family)
H 2–20m   March–April

Habitat *Wild in damp forests around the Mediterranean. Not hardy in central Europe. Flowers in clusters between leaves.*

> **foliage and fruits have a strong tangy aroma when crushed**
> **can trigger allergies**
> **often grown as a decorative pot plant**

Laurel wreaths crowned the heads of the victorious Julius Caesar and other Roman commanders. In Greece, successful athletes were also awarded this decoration. Later, students were honoured with the 'baccalaureus', a laurel wreath with berries. The academic title of Bachelor was derived from this.

crown rounded to oval

form very dense

mostly multiple stems

evergreen, lighter below

margin wavy

leaf 5–10cm long, slender, elliptic

fruit 1–1.5cm in size

green when unripe, glossy black when ripe

Camphor Laurel

Cinnamomum camphora (bay family)
H 5–40m   March–July

Camphor Laurel crops are grown in Japan and Taiwan. All parts of the tree contain camphor, but in varying quantities. Only the wood from trees aged at least 50 or 60 years supplies a worthwhile yield. Camphor is used medicinally, but can also be poisonous, depending on the quantity. Camphor ointments are therefore not suitable for infants and should only be used with caution on young children.

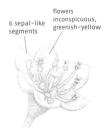

6 sepal-like segments

flowers inconspicuous, greenish-yellow

Habitat Native to east Asia. Often in parks and avenues in the Mediterranean. Easily recognisable by the characteristically veined leaves.

> crushed leaves typically smell of camphor
> evergreen
> newly sprouting leaves reddish

dark green above

matt blue-green below

leaf 6–12cm long

leaf veins curved

Did you know?

Natural camphor is sold on the market as powdery crystals or in the form of colourless to white pieces, which have a pungent smell. The substance deters moths. It is used in cold remedies to soothe coughs and in rheumatism ointments to ease pain.

67

crown broadly oval

projecting branches

Quince

Cydonia oblonga (rose family)
H 4–6m May–June

flower around 5cm in size

5 petals

Habitat Native to west Asia; arrived in southern Europe more than 2,500 years ago, later came to central Europe. Fruits can also be pear-shaped.

> needs sufficient warmth
> fruit ripens in October or November
> several cultivated varieties

In ancient times, Quince fruits (quinces) were consecrated to Aphrodite. The 'Apples of Cydonia' symbolised love and fertility. Greek brides and bridegrooms were therefore required by law to eat a quince before their wedding night... Ripe quinces have an intensive, fruity, aromatic scent. The hard, bitter, sour fruits do not taste pleasant raw, but make excellent juice and jelly.

fruit up to 15cm long, felted, hairy

bloom can be wiped off ripe fruits

often apple-shaped

leaf 5–15cm long, oval

matt green above

felted and hairy below

crown broadly spreading

trunk short or shrub-like with multiple stems

Did you know?

In Greek mythology, Hercules had to obtain the 'golden apples of the Hesperides' as one of his twelve labours. He completed the task and received golden quinces as a reward. The 'apple of Venus' was in reality a quince.

Willow-leafed Pear

Pyrus salicifolia (rose family)

H 5–9m   April

The Willow-leafed Pear is an attractive alternative to other silver-leafed trees in gardens, such as the Oleaster (p. 72) or White Willow (p. 82). It grows fairly slowly and thus only requires little space. In spring, it is often covered in an abundance of flowers. Its fruits are unpleasant to eat.

Habitat *Native to Asia Minor. In gardens in Europe. White flowers in florets with multiple flowers.*

> foliage bright silver
> leaves similar to those of the White Willow (p. 82)
> fruits remain hard

twigs thin, fairly pendulous

fruit is a 2–3cm long, rounded, green, spotted pear

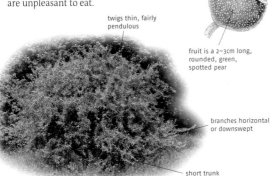

branches horizontal or downswept

short trunk

leaf up to 9cm long, very slender, elliptic

often silvery grey initially, later green

silvery grey below

Cherry Laurel

Prunus laurocerasus (rose family)

H 1–6m May

cluster erect, up to 20cm long

flowers around 8mm in size

The evergreen leaves are similar to those of the Bay Laurel (p. 66) and the fruits resemble cherries (p. 100). The species is in fact related to cherries. Unlike these, however, all parts of this plant are poisonous, containing noxious substances that release prussic acid. When the leaves are crushed or the bark peeled, a typical smell of bitter almonds is released.

Habitat *Wild in the Balkans and Asia Minor. Often as an ornamental and hedge shrub in central and southern Europe. Often bears ripe and unripe fruits at the same time.*

> mostly grows as a shrub in gardens
> sometimes flowers a second time in autumn
> also known as the 'Versailles Laurel'

branches ascending or spreading

spherical, pea-sized fruits

small evergreen tree or broad, bushy shrub

first red, then black when ripening

leaf 5–25cm long

shiny dark green, leathery

Judas Tree
Cercis siliquastrum (pea family)
H 3–10m May

6–15cm long, flat, hard pod

Habitat *Originally in the eastern Mediterranean. As an ornamental tree in southern and central Europe. Flowers in clusters on twigs and trunk.*

> hardy, but prefers mild locations
> one of the most popular ornamental trees in southern Europe
> fruits on the tree in winter

Back in biblical times, this tree ornamented the gardens of Judea and, according to legend, Judas hanged himself from one. The flowers were supposedly white originally, taking on their pink hue after the crucifixion of Christ. The flowers can be used to garnish salads, but the fruits are inedible.

crown broadly spreading, often irregular

leaf up to 11cm long, round to kidney-shaped

base heart-shaped

pea-like flowers up to 2cm long, pink

rough, leathery, hairless

generally with multiple stems

70

Alder Buckthorn
Frangula alnus (buckthorn family)
H 1.5–5m   May–July

branches mostly steeply angled

crown very sparse, often broad further up

Habitat *Wild through-out most of Europe in riverside forests, on moors and in sparse forests. Also planted to stabilise river banks. Usually produces abundant fruit.*

> leaves alternate
> needs damp or wet soil
> bark smells rotten

Alder Buckthorn bark is a well-known laxative, which takes effect reliably after a few hours. Owing to possible side-effects, however, it must only be taken in small quantities and for a short period of time. The twigs once supplied charcoal for the manufacture of gunpowder.

leaf veins curved
matt green

often fruits at different stages of maturity together

stone fruits around 8mm in size

leaves 2–5cm long, broadly elliptic

tree or large shrub

Tasmanian Blue Gum

Eucalyptus globulus (myrtle family)

H 10–45m   December–May

These trees take up large amounts of water from underground and evaporate it through the leaves. They are therefore planted to drain swampy areas. In the Tropics, this plays a special role in areas where malaria occurs. The larvae of mosquitoes that carry the virus are often dependent on areas of open water. If these sites disappear, there is less 'swamp fever'. The intensively aromatic oil from the leaves is used as a cough remedy.

Habitat *Native to Australia. Often planted in the Mediterranean, also in the streets. Flowers with numerous stamens.*

> **crushed leaves smell of cough sweets**
> **grows rapidly**
> **evergreen**

fruit lopsided and conical

leaves hanging downwards

slender crown

leaves on young trees elongated and oval

blue-green

surround stem

71

flowers 3–4cm wide

leaves dark green, leathery

flowers open with a lid

leaves on old trees up to 15cm long, sickle-shaped

bark detaches in strips

Did you know?

Although eucalyptus forests are very light, there is no life in them. Inhibitors produced by the trees suppress the growth of many other plants, which would be necessary to support fauna.

Oleaster

Elaeagnus angustifolia (sea-buckthorn family)
H 6–8m June

yellow to yellowish-brown when ripe

leaf silvery-white below

olive-like fruits, around 1cm long

crown has various forms, often broad and uneven

Habitat Native to western and central Asia. Naturalised in the Mediterranean, in parks of central Europe. Bears abundant inconspicuous fruits.

> twigs often have thorns
> similar to the White Willow (p. 82)
> fruit rarely ripens in northern Europe

leaf up to 8cm long, slender and elongated

matt green above

The Oleaster only grows as an ornamental tree or in windbreak hedges in many areas. However, a variety with larger fruits, which are sold at markets, is found from the eastern Mediterranean to central Asia. The fruits have a sweet taste and can be processed to make compote, jam and liqueurs. A fatty oil can be pressed from the seeds.

numerous branches

one or more stems, often twisted

4 yellow petals

small flowers

Crepe Myrtle

Lagerstroemia indica (purple loosestrife family)
H 2–8m July–September

flowers around 3cm in size

usually 6 crumpled petals

petals with stems

Habitat Native to Asia. In parks and gardens in southern Europe, as a pot plant in central Europe. Abundant flowers at ends of twigs.

> petals like crepe paper
> flowers pink, red, violet or white
> highly decorative ornamental tree

stem short or missing

leaf 2–7cm long, elliptic or elongated

The Crepe Myrtle needs plenty of warmth to produce abundant flowers. In central Europe, it should be placed in a pot directly in front of a south-facing wall. In the south, it grows extremely well without much care required, even in the street. This distinctive tree has many named varieties, such as the 'Red Rocket' and 'Delta Blush'.

flowers at ends of twigs

rounded crown

one or more stems

Pomegranate

Punica granatum (pomegranate family)

H 2–7m May–September

With their many distinctive seeds, pomegranates were consecrated to the gods of fertility in ancient times. But they also symbolised hope of reincarnation – a symbol that the Christian church took over and depicted in pictures and on robes. Juice can be pressed from the juicy outer layer of the seeds to make grenadine syrup. The peel supplies a natural yellow to red-brown dye for carpets.

Habitat Native to central Asia. In commercial plantations and gardens around the Mediterranean. Distinctive, bright flowers.

> extremely old cultivated plant
> red seed casing has a sour taste
> a dwarf form exists with smaller leaves and flowers

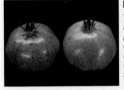

Did you know?

The first hand grenades developed in the Middle Ages resembled pomegranates. Both names are derived from the Latin 'grana', meaning 'grains'. The hollow-barrelled weapons broke into many small pieces when they exploded.

leaf 2–7cm long, lanceolate

glossy green

leathery peel

fruit up to 12cm thick, apple-shaped

seeds with a juicy, red casing

73

abundant branches

mostly multiple stems

Giant Dogwood
Cornus controversa (dogwood family)
H 8–10m May–June

around 6mm thick

fruits blue–black
when ripe

The storey-like structure of the tree is reminiscent
of pagodas in eastern Asian temples. As well as
the green-leafed species, a cultivar, which has leaves with white
margins, can be found, particularly in French and
Italian parks. Birds eat the fruit in autumn
and excrete the seeds undigested.

Habitat *Naturally
occurring from the east-
ern Himalayas to Korea
and Japan. In parks
and squares in Europe.
Beautiful in autumn
too with its yellow to
red leaf colour.*

> unlike the other
  dogwood species, the
  leaves are alternate
> attractive as a single tree
> fruit attracts birds

branches
horizontal

arranged
in striking
storeys

flowers
small,
white

clusters up to
18cm wide

curved leaf
veins

leaf up to 12cm
long, broadly
oval

74

Japanese Dogwood
Cornus kousa (dogwood family)
H 4–6m ay–June

tiny flowers

What looks like a flower is actually a whole
cluster surrounded by four showy bracts.
While the tiny flowers are developing, these
bracts slowly change from green to white.
The similar Flowering Dogwood is native
to North America. This also comes with
pink bracts.

Habitat *Native to
Japan and Korea. In
parks and gardens in
Europe. Storey-shaped
form with hanging
leaves and flowers.*

> turns scarlet in autumn
> prefers acidic soils
> highly decorative tree

3–5cm
long,
pointed

4 bracts

branches horizontal

form broadly spreading

curved
leaf veins

long and
pointed

leaf 6–9cm long

Cornelian Cherry

Cornus mas (dogwood family)
H 3–8m   March–April

The wood of the Cornelian Cherry is extremely tough and hard. In ancient times, it was used to make shafts for lances. The lance which Romulus used to mark out the city border when founding Rome was allegedly made of Cornelian Cherry wood. Bicycle spokes, tools and wooden nails were often made from this wood. The fruit stones were roasted to make ersatz coffee or threaded to form simple rosaries.

flowers around 5 mm in size, yellow

10–25 together

Habitat In sunny copses, sparse forests and on embankments in central and southern Europe. Flowers long before foliation.

> leaves opposite
> attractive, early-flowering ornamental tree
> useful for bees and birds

Did you know?

The fruits are known as 'Dirndln' in Austria, like the traditional dress, and are a real insider tip for lovers of wild fruit. Jams made from the ripe, sour fruits have a similar flavour to woodland strawberries and rose hips.

lighter below

leaf up to 8cm long, broad and lanceolate

mostly 4 pairs of curved leaf veins

stone fruit up to 2cm long, bright red when ripe

75

generally unevenly rounded in outline

branches usually very squarrose

one or more stems

Japanese Persimmon
Diospyros kaki (ebony family)
H 5–15m   une

Habitat Native to Japan, South Korea and China. Cultivated as a fruit tree in the Mediterranean. Unripe fruits hidden beneath the leaves.

> sensitive to frost
> fruits only taste really good when overripe
> several hundred varieties known worldwide

Japanese Persimmon fruits, which are also known as 'sharon fruit', contain so much vitamin A that adults can meet their daily requirements with one or two fruits. Some varieties taste sweet and similar to apricots, while others are bitter and astringent, leaving a furry feeling in the mouth. The fruits are mostly eaten raw, but can also be used in compotes, jams and cakes.

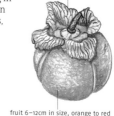

4 large sepals

fruit 6–12cm in size, orange to red

flower up to 1.5cm wide, yellowish-white

sepals far larger than petals

glossy above

lighter below, hairy

leaf up to 16cm long

Did you know?
The fruits of most persimmons develop without pollination and thus do not contain any stones. It is impossible to tell whether they will taste sweet or astringent just by looking at them.

crown usually rounded

Date Plum

Diospyros lotus (ebony family)

H 5–12m   June

reddish or greenish-white

flower around 0.5 cm in size, bell-shaped

The fruits of the Date Plum are very popular, especially in eastern Asia. The Chinese and Japanese eat them raw or dried and make syrup from them. If untreated, they taste highly astringent. But if dipped in hot water for a few minutes, they become sweet.

round crown

dense foliage

fruit 1–3cm in size

yellow to blue-black, pruinose

4 large sepals

glossy

leaf 6–12cm long

Habitat *Native from south-west Asia to Japan. Around the Mediterranean, sometimes naturalised, sometimes planted. Usually produces abundant fruit.*

> **also known as the 'Lotus Tree'**
> **hardy in warm areas of central Europe**
> **fruits can only be kept a short time**

77

Foxglove Tree

Paulownia tomentosa (figwort family)

H 10–15m   April–May

flowers funnel-shaped, blue-violet

One of the shields of the Japanese imperial family bears leaves and flowers of the Foxglove Tree in a stylised form. The tree, which is also known as the 'Empress Tree', is not only decorative when in flower. In the past, it was often kept purely as a leafy plant and the shoots were regularly cut down to the ground. This produced shoots up to four metres high with leaves of up to 50 centimetres in size.

crown broad to umbrella-like

some strong branches

fruits up to 4cm long, oval

pointed

short trunk

leaf up to 25cm long, broadly oval to heart-shaped

hairy

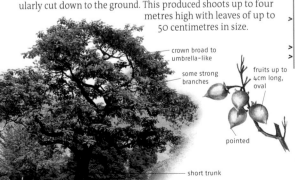

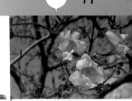

Habitat *Native to China. In parks of southern and central Europe. Eye-catching in spring with its unusually coloured flowers.*

> **young trees and flower buds sensitive to heavy frost**
> **tolerates air pollution**
> **fruits often remain on the tree all winter**

Indian Bean Tree

Catalpa bignonioides (bignonia family)
H 15–18m   June–July

Habitat Native to eastern North America. In parks and gardens in Europe. Distinctive flowers up to 20cm long.

> fruits often remain on the tree for months
> leaves have an unpleasant scent when crushed
> grows fairly quickly

Bees and bumblebees swarm over the richly flowering trees, often in large numbers. The lower lip of the flowers offers the insects an attractive landing place. From there, they crawl into the floral tubes to reach the sweet, well-hidden nectar.

flower up to 5cm long

with a yellow and violet pattern

stem up to 15cm long

heart-shaped

leaf blade 10–15cm long

branches often horizontal or downswept

strong branches

crown broadly spreading, often uneven

78

fruit up to 30cm long and 1cm thick

opens lengthwise

Did you know?

The fruits release large quantities of seeds. These have long wings ending in hairs, which allow them to float well on the air and be blown over long distances by the wind.

Olive

Olea europaea (olive family)
H 5–15m   May–June

The Olive tree was utilised by ancient peoples. The oil pressed from almost fully mature olives is a valuable ingredient in the healthy Mediterranean diet. Good edible oil is pressed from ground fruits without heating (cold). Warm-pressed oil is of a poorer quality, while hot-pressed oil is only suitable for technical purposes.

Habitat *All around the Mediterranean region. Wild form in forests and copses. Fruits ripen from green to red-brown or black.*

> *can live more than 1,000 years*
> *branch is a symbol of peace*
> *supplies oil and olives*

crown broadly spreading

branches mostly thick

4 petals

flower just a few millimetres in size

fruit up to 3.5cm long

leaf 4–6cm long, leathery

dark green above

silvery grey below

trunk often gnarled

blue-black when ripe

79

Canary Island Dragon Tree

Dracaena draco (lily family)
H 3–20m   July–August

It is extremely difficult to estimate the age of dragon trees because they do not have any rings that can be counted. However, today's botanists know that the trees reach a maximum of 400 years of age – not several thousand, as scientists previously believed. Damage to the trunk causes a red resin to flow out: the 'dragon's blood'.

Habitat *Native only to the Canary Islands. Commonly grown there. Branched clusters with berries between tufts of leaves.*

> *rarely found in the wild*
> *flowers just once every 15 years*
> *grows for many years without branching*

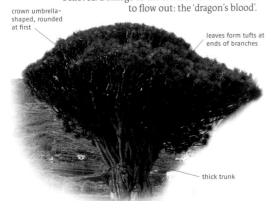

crown umbrella-shaped, rounded at first

leaves form tufts at ends of branches

leaf grey-green

up to 60cm long, sword-shaped, firm

pyramidal base

thick trunk

Goat Willow

Salix caprea (willow family)
H 2–10m   March–May

Habitat *Wild throughout most of Europe in clearings, on edges of forests, in gravel pits and quarries. Male catkins particularly distinctive.*

> *male and female trees*
> *tolerates wet and dry soils*
> *also grown as a hanging variety in gardens*

The Goat Willow flowers early and produces large quantities of nectar, making it one of the first rich sources of food for bees in spring. People should therefore take care not to cut too many twigs as decorations. On Palm Sunday, Goat Willow twigs are often used in central Europe as a substitute for the palm fronds of the south. This has given rise to the tree's alternative name of 'Palm Willow' as well as the occasional use of 'Willow Sunday' to mean Palm Sunday in Britain.

leaves 3–10cm long

margin crenate, wavy or smooth

relatively wrinkled

often has stipules

Did you know?

The strong, brown bud scales often break open on the first warm days of the year. The sensitive flowers are still well-protected from frost by dense hairs – these are the catkins with their soft, silvery grey fur.

yellow anthers

flowers in catkins of up to 4cm in length, appear before foliage

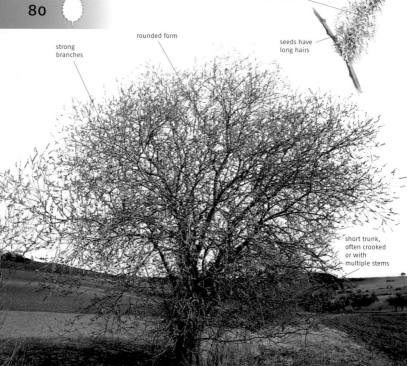

fertile catkin

seeds have long hairs

rounded form

strong branches

short trunk, often crooked or with multiple stems

Weeping Willow

Salix babylonica (willow family)
H 8–12m   April–May

Willows often ornament the shores of lakes and ponds in parks. Some of these are the true Weeping Willow, which was introduced to Europe more than 200 years ago and has particularly long twigs – however, most are hybrids, which are difficult to distinguish from one another.

Habitat Native from the Caucasus to China. In parks and gardens in Europe. Both male and female catkins are characteristically curved.

> - highly distinctive ornamental tree
> - sensitive to heavy frosts
> - often cultivated as hybrids with similar forms

crown often broader than it is high

long twigs hang down vertically

male flowers in curved, thin catkins

leaf up to 16cm long, slender and lanceolate

margin finely serrated

Corkscrew Willow

Salix matsudana 'tortuosa' (willow family)
H 4–8m   March–April

The Corkscrew Willow is one of the easiest species of willow to identify. It grows extremely quickly and therefore requires sufficient space if planted in a garden. It can be propagated easily – it is enough to place a twig in water and wait for the roots to grow.

branches upswept

Habitat Undemanding variety of an east Asian willow, only as a cultivar. In parks and gardens in Europe. Characteristic twisted twigs.

> - popular in floral art
> - beautiful appearance in winter due to contorted form
> - the Corkscrew Hazel (p. 198) also has twisted twigs

branches and twigs twisted like corkscrews

leaf 5–8cm long, slender and lanceolate

usually curved

White Willow

Salix alba (willow family)
H 8–20m   April–May

Habitat *Wild throughout most of Europe on banks of rivers and streams, lake shores and in riverside forests. Leaves often a distinctive, shiny silver.*

> largest and most frequently found native willow
> grows up to 2m per year
> flowers at the same time as foliation

The White Willow forms a dense, flat system of roots, which it uses to stabilise river banks. It can also be planted in flood-prone areas because it can stand in water for weeks at a time. Old trees are often hollow since the wood weathers rapidly. These hollows are used as a hiding place by birds, small mammals and other animals or become filled with humus and serve as natural 'flower pots' for other plants.

Did you know?

The flexible, thin twigs of the White Willow are suitable for weaving like those of the Osier (p. 62). Trees that are pruned regularly grow into impressive pollarded willows with thick trunks.

leaf 5–8cm long, slender and lanceolate

dense, silvery hairs below

sparsely haired above

82

crown conical initially, later high-domed

numerous branches

male flowers in yellow catkins, up to 7cm long

branches spreading

female catkins greenish

Crack Willow

Salix fragilis (willow family)
H 5–15m   April–May

The twigs of the Crack Willow snap off easily at the base, unlike those of the White Willow (p. 82), and with an audible cracking sound. But like the White Willow, the tree can be planted on river banks to prevent erosion during high water.

crown broad, rounded

male flowers in yellow, cylindrical catkins

branches and twigs often almost horizontal

female catkins green

long-stemmed

one or more stems

Habitat *Wild throughout most of Europe by streams, ditches, riverbanks and in alder forests. Leaves have clearly distinguishable upper and lower sides.*

> *also known as 'Withy'*
> *needs damp to wet soil*
> *can be crossed with the White Willow*

leaf up to 18cm long

glossy dark green above

margin with cartilaginous teeth

Balsam Poplar

Populus balsamifera (willow family)
H 20–30m   March–April

The Balsam Poplar is the most northerly growing deciduous tree in America. Its northern boundary runs along the tree line from Newfoundland to Alaska. As a light-loving pioneer tree, it colonises recently flooded ground along rivers and lakes.

straight trunk far up into the crown

slender form

Habitat *Native to northern North America. In parks and avenues and by rivers in Europe. Underside of leaf typically whitish or yellowish.*

> *buds and young shoots smell of balsam*
> *buds sticky*
> *cut twigs can grow roots*

leaf 5–12cm long, heart-shaped or oval

margin crenate and serrated

fairly rough

Carolina Poplar
Populus x *canadensis* (willow family)
H 20–30m   March–April

Habitat Hybrids between European and North American Black Poplars; grown frequently. Bark deeply furrowed.

> also known as a 'Canadian Poplar'
> leaves often reddish as shoots
> can trigger skin allergies, as can the propolis produced from it

These trees grow extremely quickly and supply soft wood, which is used to make cellulose. Bees gather the sticky drops from poplar buds and other trees and then mix them with saliva and wax. They use the resulting propolis to seal cracks in their hives. The ancient Egyptians used this substance to embalm their mummies. Today, there are countless propolis-based products on the market for treating skin diseases and promoting vitality.

crown slender to broadly conical

branches project at a sharp angle from trunk, upswept

leaf 7–10cm long, fairly triangular

usually has glands at base of stem

flattened stem

84

up to 8cm long, hanging

male catkins red

Did you know?
The different varieties of Carolina Poplar can only be propagated using roots grown from twigs and not with seeds. All trees that are planted therefore have the same genetic make-up and also the same uniform shape.

Black Poplar

Populus nigra (willow family)
H 15–30m   March–April

Poplar seeds have a tuft of thin white hairs, which allows them to fly as far as 15 kilometres. However, they have to find a suitable landing place quickly because they can only germinate for one to two weeks. To make sure they reproduce, the trees form huge quantities of seeds, which often lie on the ground like wool. Scientists have calculated that each tree can produce over 25 million seeds per year.

Habitat *Wild in riverside forests and by backwaters in northern and central Europe. Varieties in parks and fields. Leaves often distinctively diamond-shaped.*

> *young leaves already green*
> *tolerates floods*
> *sawn-off trunks and stumps produce new shoots*

Did you know?
The Lombardy Poplar (Populus nigra 'Italica') is a cultivar of the Black Poplar, which was known as far back as the early Middle Ages. Since Napoleon's times, it has been grown frequently in Germany because he ordered it to be planted along avenues. Nearly all the trees are male and are propagated by growing roots from twigs.

leaf diamond-shaped, 5–10cm long

long and pointed

no glands at base of stem

85

crown broad, sparse

strong branches

female catkins green

male catkins red

5–8cm long

seeds with white hairs

Aspen

Populus tremula (willow family)
H 10–30m   March–April

Habitat *Wild throughout most of Europe in sparse forests, clearings, on rocks and by roadsides. Turns golden-yellow to orange-red in autumn.*

> often forms dense groups due to shoots from the roots
> needs plenty of light
> colonises newly created sites as a pioneer plant

blade 3–8cm long, round to broadly oval

blunt teeth on margin

stem generally longer than blade, flattened

male catkins with shaggy, grey hairs

The expression 'to tremble like an Aspen leaf' comes from the long leaf stalks, which are flattened sideways: just a tiny breath of air is enough to cause a fluttering among the leaves. People once believed that the incessant rustling sound of the leaves was a lament and therefore thought that the Aspen was a tree of the Underworld.

slender crown

branches spaced out, often irregular

female catkins greenish

86

Italian Alder

Alnus cordata (birch family)
H 10–15m   March–April

Habitat *Native to Corsica and southern Italy only. Grown in central and western Europe. Leaves characteristically heart-shaped and noticeably shiny.*

> excellent pioneer species
> tolerates aridity
> largest cone-like fruits of all alder trees

heart-shaped

leaf 4–10cm long, leathery

lighter below, with brown hairs

The Italian Alder is fairly undemanding and is even grown by the roadside in city centres. In central Europe, it also provides shade in some shopping streets and squares. The leaves barely change colour in autumn, but remain on the twigs for a long time.

form conical to oval

straight trunk

cone-like fruits up to 3cm long

often persist on the tree in winter

Black Alder
Alnus glutinosa (birch family)
H 10–25m   January–April

The Black Alder has soft wood, which is highly resistant to water and has therefore been used in hydraulic engineering and earthworks for many years. Many sluice gates were made of Alder wood in the past. If the bark comes into contact with iron in water, the water turns a deep black after a few days. Saddlers and cobblers once used this liquid to dye their leather. Fallen leaves also turn black under water.

fruits on the side have clear stems

multiple cone-like fruits, up to 2cm long

Habitat Wild throughout most of Europe in riverside forests, water meadows, by streams and springs. Wood has a distinctive rust red colour.

> *flowers before foliation*
> *roots grow down to 4m*
> *high groundwater level*

crown sparse, conical to oval

trunk reaches far up into the crown

notched at apex

leaf 4–10cm long, oval to rounded

87

female catkins up to 1cm long, reddish

male catkins up to 8cm long

yellowish when opened

one or often more stems

Did you know?

Nodules containing bacteria form on alder roots. These growths are apple-sized, grape-like and woody. The bacteria absorb nitrogen from the air and thus supply the tree with this valuable element.

Grey Alder

Alnus incana (birch family)
H 8–20m   March–April

fruits on the side with short stems or sessile

multiple cone-like fruits, around 1.5cm long

Habitat *Wild in northern and central Europe in riverside forests and on banks of streams. Often planted. Leaves pointed, unlike those of the Black Alder.*

> tolerates both dry and wet locations
> does not change colour in autumn
> named after the colour of the bark

Along mountain streams and Alpine rivers, the Grey Alder often forms large stands and can be identified by its grey trunk, particularly in winter. Outside the mountains, it is grown as a tolerant windbreak tree and to improve the appearance of rubbish tips. It produces shoots easily from sawn-off stumps and then forms large shrubs.

crown uneven and conical

branches mostly ascending

leaf pointed at tip

margin with large, finely serrated teeth

4–10cm long, oval to elliptic

one or more stems

bark white-grey

Downy Birch

Betula pubescens (birch family)
H 5–20m   April–May

bark smooth on almost the whole tree

Habitat *Wild on moors, in moor woodlands and swamps in northern and central Europe. Distinguished from the Silver Birch by its oval leaves.*

> very shallow roots
> highly resistant to frost
> unlike the Silver Birch, it also grows in the few forests on Iceland

The Downy Birch was one of the first trees to recolonise central Europe after the last Ice Age. Today, the moorlands that are suitable for the tree are sometimes a long way apart. Thanks to its flying seeds, however, it can disperse itself over distances of several kilometres on the wind.

bright white with horizontal bands

crown sparse, conical to rounded

twigs do not hang or only hang slightly

branches upswept or horizontal

female catkins erect

leaf 3–5cm long, oval

serrated margin

young leaves hairy on top

male catkins up to 8cm long

Silver Birch

Betula pendula (birch family)
H 8–25m   April–May

Before the various plastics took over, the Silver Birch tree played a diverse role. The light but tough wood was used to make propellers, aircraft wings, skis, sledge runners, wheel rims, sports equipment and cotton reels. The sap, which flows out of wounds on the tree trunk before foliation, is still used in revitalising cures and hair tonics. Tea made from the leaves is an excellent kidney tonic.

fertile catkins decay when ripe

Habitat *Native throughout most of Europe in forests, clearings, on heaths and wasteland. Bark bright white with dark bosses and fissures.*

> *also known as the 'Lady of the Woods' or 'Warty Birch'*
> *needs plenty of light*
> *pollen triggers hay fever*

crown elongated, sparse

leaf 3–7cm long, triangular to diamond-shaped

double row of teeth on margin

branches mostly projecting from trunk at a sharp angle

twigs thin, usually hanging

89

female catkins green to reddish, erect

male catkins up to 10cm long, hanging

Did you know?

The Masur or Karelian Birch is a special form of Silver Birch, producing beautifully patterned wood, which is valued for small furniture and woodturning work.

River Birch
Betula nigra (birch family)
H 15–20m   April–May

Habitat *Native to the eastern United States. In parks and gardens in Europe. Bark red-brown to black, curling.*

> **dark bark, unlike on other birch trees**
> **foliage yellow in autumn**
> **needs plenty of space in a garden**

The River Birch grows wild in its natural habitat in the eastern United States by rivers and lakes as well as in swamps. This is why it is also known as the 'Water Birch'. The tree is planted to protect damp and wet soils from eroding away in many places throughout the United States. In Europe, it is only grown as an exotic tree in parks and gardens.

crown conical to rounded, sparse

multiple stems or thick branches

bark on young trunks still smooth and shiny

leaf 4–9cm long, diamond-shaped to oval

glossy above

White-barked Himalayan Birch
Betula utilis var. *jacquemontii* (birch family)
H 15–20m   April–May

Habitat *Native to the western Himalayas. Mostly in parks in Europe. Highly distinctive owing to the almost smooth, white bark.*

> **beautiful, particularly as a single tree**
> **foliage golden-yellow in autumn**
> **very undemanding**

branches steeply ascending

The white of the bark is caused by the dye betulin, which reflects sunlight and thus prevents it from heating up. This is important for free-standing trees on cold winter days: on dark barks, the difference in temperature between the sunny and shady sides can cause the trunks to split open. A chalk coating on fruit trees serves the same purpose.

leaf 5–7.5cm long, pointed oval

dark green above

double row of teeth on margin

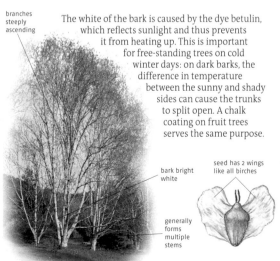

bark bright white

seed has 2 wings like all birches

generally forms multiple stems

Common Hornbeam

Carpinus betulus (birch family)

H 5–25m May

appear simultaneously with leaves

female catkins inconspicuous

The Common Hornbeam is not closely related to the Common Beech (p. 60), although often confused with it. The name 'hornbeam' was derived from the wood's use in making yokes for oxen – hence the tree's other name of 'Yoke Elm'. The wood is the heaviest of all native trees and is also very hard and tough. It is useful for heavily used devices, such as smoothing planes, chopping blocks, spokes and piano hammers.

male catkins 4–5cm long, hanging

Habitat Wild, particularly in deciduous forests, hedgerows and forest edges in central Europe. Frequently planted. Dry leaves often remain on trees for a long time.

> very deep roots
> fruits often blown off by the wind in winter
> also known as the 'European Hornbeam'

trunk has characteristic lengthwise bosses and fissures

blade has corrugated texture due to prominent leaf veins

Did you know?

The Common Hornbeam tolerates strong pruning and grows back densely, making it a popular hedge tree. It is also used as a remedy to treat exhaustion and weariness.

hard nut-like fruits

each has a wing up to 4cm long

double-toothed margin

leaf 5–11cm long, oval

91

crown conical initially, later broadly spreading

often has strong branches down to the ground

rounded above

one or more stems

European Hop Hornbeam

Ostrya carpinifolia (birch family)
H 10–20m   April–May

crown conical or
ovate to rounded

Habitat Wild in mixed forests from southern Europe to Asia Minor. In parks of central Europe. Hop-like fruits.

> form and leaves resemble those of the Common Hornbeam (p. 91)
> tolerates aridity
> needs sufficient warmth

The scientific name *Ostrya* was derived from the Greek name for oysters. The sack-like shells around the nut fruits slightly resemble oyster shells. These act as a wing for the fruits, which only works well in strong winds and can transport the seeds over long distances.

male catkins
up to 10cm long,
yellow-brown

fruit 3–6cm
long

leaf 4–10cm
long, oval

double-
toothed
margin

elongated tip

one or
more stems

each nut-like fruit
has a parchment-
like shell

Turkish Hazel

Corylus colurna (birch family)
H 10–20m   February–March

crown usually very
regular and conical

Habitat Native to southern Europe and Asia Minor. Frequently in streets and parks in central Europe. Produces very hard-shelled filberts.

> fruits form ball-like tufts
> unlike the Hazel (p. 198), it has just one trunk
> also known as the 'Turkish Filbert'

The nuts of the Turkish Hazel taste similar to those of the Hazel (p. 198). However, they are difficult to crack and very small. The beautifully grained wood is excellent for furniture and carving, as indicated by the species name *colurna*. This means 'made of hazel wood'.

trunk straight
right up to tip

male catkins up
to 12cm long

female flower
with red stigmas

leaf 8–12cm long,
broadly oval

base heart-
shaped

double-toothed margin

brown nut-
like fruit

enclosed in a
deeply slit,
sticky shell

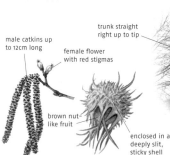

Cork Oak

Quercus suber (beech family)

H 6–10m   April–May

This tree is grown in plantations to produce cork, particularly in southern Portugal and the south of Spain. The trunks are peeled for the first time once they have reached an age of 15 to 20 years. This does not harm the tree since it is just dead material. The cork covering takes around ten years to regenerate sufficiently to be harvested again. The natural product cork has been in great demand over the past years, especially for building environmentally friendly homes.

Did you know?

To make sure that the cork is not airtight around the tree, air channels run inwards, which are filled with loose powder. Corks for bottles are therefore only cut lengthwise to the surface, thus preventing the wine from escaping through the channels.

Habitat Widespread in the central and western Mediterranean. Cultivated for many years. Characteristically thick, fissured cork bark.

> evergreen
> trunks turn dark red the first year after peeling
> only as a pot plant in central Europe

leaf 3–7cm long, leathery

margin with 3–6 teeth on each side

dark green above

grey, felted below

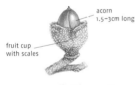

acorn 1.5–3cm long

fruit cup with scales

crown sparse, generally broadly domed

93

branches often thick

Sweet Chestnut

Castanea sativa (beech family)
H 10–30m   June–July

catkins up to 15cm long

Habitat In forests in southern Europe, and wine-growing areas and parks in Germany. Closed spiny shells resembling little hedgehogs.

> *flowers have an unpleasant aroma*
> *not related to the Horse Chestnut (p. 155)*
> *naturalised by the Romans north of the Alps*

The fruits of this tree were a staple foodstuff in many areas of southern Europe as recently as the 19th century. The trees were grown in large coppices for this purpose. The wood is resistant to moisture and can be used to make staves, stable floors and ships. To make vine stakes, vintners would often cut off 15–20-year old trunks. The stumps then produced shoots again and grew into slender trees with multiple stems.

abundant male flowers

leaf up to 30cm long, elongated, lanceolate

margin roughly serrated

firm, slightly leathery

fruit casing opens with 4 flaps when ripe

spiny shell surrounding 1–3 chestnuts

few female flowers

crown broadly columnar to spherical

94

chestnut brown, smooth

Did you know?

Roasted chestnuts are sold at markets in many regions in winter, particularly at Christmas. The fruits contain a wealth of carbohydrates as well as fat, and have a sweet aromatic taste.

trunk often twisted

Antarctic Beech
Nothofagus antarctica (beech family)
H 5–7m   April–May

In the wild, all Antarctic Beech trees grow exclusively in the
southern hemisphere, as the name suggests. In central Europe,
the tree is suitable for small gardens where it catches the eye with
its often twisted form and small leaves. The tree also
forms strong stems in its natural habitat and its wood
is therefore usually used as fuel.

Habitat *Native to South
America, from Chile
to Tierra del Fuego. In
parks and gardens in
central Europe. Twigs
evenly covered with
small leaves.*

> **twigs often zigzag-**
  shaped
> **often develops as a shrub**
> **fruits similar to those**
  of the Common Beech
  (p. 60)

branches
upswept

crown often
irregular, bizarre,
translucent

female flowers
with red stigmas

delicate form

male flowers with
yellow stamens

leaf up to 3cm
long, oval

3 nut-like
fruits

woody fruit cup
with 4 flaps

crenate
margin

95

European Hackberry
Celtis australis (elm family)
H 10–20m   April–May

The fruit flesh tastes sweet when ripe. The fruits are not sold in
Britain, but are occasionally served in desserts in South Tyrol. The
wood is highly flexible so thin stems and twigs therefore make
excellent fishing rods and whip handles.

Habitat *Wild in
deciduous forests and
copses in southern
Europe. Often by the
roadside around the
Mediterranean. Single
fruit at each leaf axil.*

> **upper side of leaf rough,**
  unlike the following
  species
> **only relatively hardy in**
  central Europe
> **birds feed off the fruits**

single flowers
at leaf axils

form broadly
spreading

long fruit
stem

inconspicuous
flowers

spherical stone
fruit, around
1cm in size,
reddish to black
when ripe

main branches upswept

leaf 5–16cm long,
elongated to
elliptic

tip very
long

grey-green,
soft hairs below

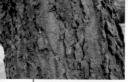

Common Hackberry

Celtis occidentalis (elm family)
H 10–25m   April–May

Habitat Native to
eastern North America.
In parks of central
Europe. Grey bark
uneven and bulging.

> foliage yellow in autumn
> tolerates cold winters
> better than the previous
> species
> common in its natural
> habitat

crown squarrose,
often irregular

The sweet fruits of the Common Hackberry are
just as edible as those of the European
Hackberry (p. 95), but have even less
fruit flesh. They often persist
on the tree all winter. In the
tree's natural habitat, they
attract more than 25 different
species of birds and small
mammals.

some branches
hanging

stone fruit
0.7–1cm in size

leaf 5–12cm long,
lopsided oval

smooth and shiny above

orange-brown
to dark crimson
when ripe

Caucasian Elm

Zelkova carpinifolia (elm family)
H 10–25m May

Habitat Native to the
Caucasus. Frequently
found in parks in
England and southern
Europe, but less often
in central Europe.
Fruits on very short
stems at leaf axils.

> foliage yellow-orange
> in autumn
> similar to the Common
> Hornbeam in terms of
> form (p. 91)
> undemanding, but only
> semi-hardy in northern
> Europe

In its native origin, the Caucasian
Elm grows in riverside forests on
the Caspian Sea. Bonsai fans
often cultivate the tree as a
bizarrely growing miniature
tree. The Caucasian Elm
tolerates severe pruning so
is also suitable as a hedge.

oval or
round crown

broom-like
form

margin
roughly
crenate

6–12 pairs
of veins

stone fruit
asymmetrical,
around 6mm in size

numerous
main branches
upswept

leaf 2–7cm
long, elliptic
and elongated

brownish when ripe

Wych Elm
Ulmus glabra (elm family)
H 20–40m   March–April

The winged fruits ripen extremely quickly and are blown away by the wind as early as May. The hard, elastic and tough wood of the Wych Elm has a beautiful grain. It supplies veneer for furniture and interior work. In ancient times, elms symbolised death and mourning.

Habitat *Throughout most of Europe in forests, hedges and on river banks. Also in parks and by the roadside. Fruits develop before foliation.*

> *flowers very early*
> *prefers cool, humid regions*
> *can live around 400 years*

Did you know?
After the First World War, many elms began dying off. Dutch Elm Disease is caused by a fungus growing inside the trees' xylem vessels. The fungus is spread by the Elm Bark Beetle, which eats characteristic galleries beneath the bark.

asymmetrical at base

often with 3 tips

very rough above

leaf 8–16cm long

97

often uneven, in several parts

crown elongated to broadly oval

red anthers

thick clusters with many flowers

fruits surrounded by flat wings

seed sitting in the centre

Small-leaved Elm

reddish flowers — *thick clusters with many short-stemmed flowers*

Ulmus minor (elm family)
H 20–35m   March–April

Habitat *Wild in copses, riverside and hilly forests throughout most of Europe. Also in parks and on roadside embankments. Branches often have raised corky ridges.*

> *highly variable form and leaf shape*
> *thrives on light and warmth*
> *indicates nutrition-rich soils*

In the past, elms took on the role of lime trees in some areas: they formed the central point of village squares and marked the spot where binding judicial rulings were made. The Small-leaved Elm can be cut back easily and therefore makes good hedges. Its leaves were once used as sheep fodder.

crown often uneven

crown conical to oval, domed

numerous branches

seed sitting in upper third

fruits elliptic, 7–15mm long

leaf usually 4–10cm long

asymmetrical base

smooth and glossy above

98

European White Elm

reddish flowers in clusters

Ulmus laevis (elm family)
H 10–35m   March–April

stems up to 15mm long

Habitat *Wild in central and eastern Europe, particularly in riverside forests. Planted by roadsides and in parks. Distinctively long stalks on fruits.*

> *fruits flutter on stalks*
> *less prone to Dutch Elm disease than other varieties*
> *also known as a 'Fluttering Elm'*

Depending on the time of year, the European White Elm can survive in flooded areas for more than 100 days without sustaining any damage. Riverside forests sometimes contain magnificent specimens. Large, board-like roots with flat sides often grow at the base of the trunk. These buttresses give the trunk greater stability in waterlogged ground.

crown elongated to broad, sparse

branches projecting diagonally from trunk

margin with lashes

flat, winged fruit

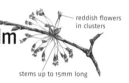

leaf up to 12cm long

underside with soft hairs

asymmetrical base

Black Mulberry

Morus nigra (mulberry family)
H 6–15m   May–June

Ripe black mulberries decay rapidly and are not often found on the market. However, those who have a chance to try the fruits, juice or jelly should definitely do so. The fruits have a sweet and sour, aromatic flavour, which is intensified by cooking. The dark juice makes a good food dye.

Habitat *Native to western Asia. Cultivated in southern Europe since ancient times. Fruits turn from white and red to black.*

> only grows into a larger tree in warm climates
> ripe fruits resemble blackberries
> contains milky sap

rounded crown

often shrub-like in Britain

often with multiple stems

short trunk

female flowers with white stigmas

fruits up to 3cm long

black when ripe, very juicy

leaf 6–20cm long

hairs on both sides

heart-shaped, occasionally lobed

99

Katsura Tree

male flower with pink stamens

Cercidiphyllum japonicum (katsura tree family)
H 5–20m   April

The Katsura Tree is one of the most important deciduous trees in the Japanese forestry industry. The light, soft wood has a beautiful grain and can be worked easily. The Japanese like to use it for small furniture, interior cladding, carving and game boards. The damp autumn leaves smell of gingerbread and biscuits.

Habitat *Native to Japan and China. Ornamental tree in gardens and parks in Europe. Foliage turns a distinctive light yellow or reddish colour in autumn.*

> some leaves opposite, some alternate
> several cultivars grown for their weeping form
> flowers before foliation

crown broadly conical to rounded

female flower with 3–5 reddish stigmas

multiple fruits together

often has multiple stems right from the ground

leaf up to 12cm long

heart-shaped

margin finely crenately serrated

Wild Cherry

Prunus avium (rose family)
H 8–20m   April–May

Habitat *Wild forms in forests and on forest edges in central Europe. Varieties cultivated throughout Europe. Supplies sweet, tasty cherries.*

> | *flowers before foliation*
> | *wild forms mostly with straight trunk right up to the tip*
> | *many cultivated varieties*

Wild Cherry fruits do not ripen after picking so they must be gathered when fully mature. The tasty fruit flesh contains a wealth of sugar, minerals and vitamins. Small cushions filled with cherry stones can be heated up in the oven or microwave and used to help ease tense muscles and rheumatism. Cherry twigs cut on 4 December – St. Barbara's Day – will flower in warm rooms, usually before Christmas.

leaf 5–15cm long, oval to elliptic

glands at base of blade

crown broadly oval to rounded

bark typically ringed

margin roughly serrated

100

branches projecting diagonally upwards

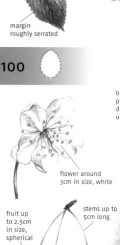

flower around 3cm in size, white

stems up to 5cm long

fruit up to 2.5cm in size, spherical

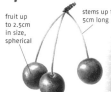

Did you know?

A mastic gum exudes from wounded trunks to seal the wounds. If boiled vigorously with water, this 'cherry gum' can soothe coughs.

Sour Cherry

Prunus cerasus (rose family)

H 3–6m   April–May

Cultivated trees do not normally grow on their own roots, but on a rootstock – often the St. Lucie Cherry (p. 104) or Cherry Plum (p. 103). Most people find fresh Sour Cherry fruits too sour. However, the cherries are popularly eaten as preserves, jams and in Black Forest gateau.

Habitat Native to western Asia. Cultivated in Europe since Roman times. Cherries light red to black-red, depending on variety.

> *varieties include 'Morello' and 'Kentish Red'*
> *flowers slightly later than Wild Cherry*
> *sour fruits*

form often shrub-like or as a trellis plant

flowers in clusters of 3–4

branches thin, fairly overhanging

leaf 5–8cm long, rough, glossy

white

usually glands at base of blade

Japanese Cherry

Prunus serrulata (rose family)

H 3–12m   April–May

crown often oval or funnel-shaped

The Japanese have been cultivating the Japanese Cherry for two millennia and have bred countless varieties. Like the equally richly blossoming ornamental cherries, the Japanese prize this as a herald of spring and celebrate its flowering with a special cherry blossom festival called 'Hanami'.

Habitat Wild forms in eastern Asia. In gardens and parks in Asia and in Europe. Some varieties also have large, unfilled flowers.

> *also known as the 'Oriental Cherry'*
> *a wealth of different varieties*
> *does not produce edible cherries*

form shrub or tree-like depending on variety

flower usually filled

up to 5cm in size

leaf 6–12cm long

stalk with glands

margin with pointed, bristly teeth

Bird Cherry
Prunus padus (rose family)
H 3–12m April–May

Habitat Wild throughout most of Europe in riverside forests and on wet edges of woods. Generally forms abundant clusters.

> needs plenty of moisture in the soil
> flowers have a pleasant scent
> fruits bitter and astringent

The bark of the tree has an unpleasant, rotten, slightly vinegary smell. The Norwegians once used it as a dye. If gathered in autumn, it dyes wool orange or dark brown, depending on the pre-treatment. Basket weavers in Russia use the flexible, olive or red-brown twigs for weaving.

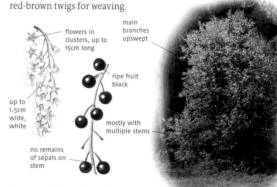

crown slender and oval to rounded

main branches upswept

flowers in clusters, up to 15cm long

ripe fruit black

mostly with multiple stems

2 glands on leaf stalk

up to 1.5cm wide, white

no remains of sepals on stem

leaf 6–12cm long, oval to elliptic

x

102

ripe fruit black, up to 1cm thick

Black Cherry
Prunus serotina (rose family)
H 5–12m May–June

remains of sepals on end of stalk

Habitat Native to eastern North America. Planted in Europe, naturalised in some areas. Hanging clusters with abundant fruits.

> very undemanding
> flowers around 2 weeks later than Bird Cherry
> fruits edible but bitter

In 1623, the Black Cherry became one of the first American tree species to be imported to Europe as an ornamental tree for gardens and parks. Forest rangers also like to use it as a windbreak, to prevent soil erosion and to improve the quality of humus. Conservationists view the tree in a critical light as it is intruding on heaths and wetlands and thereby altering the natural landscapes.

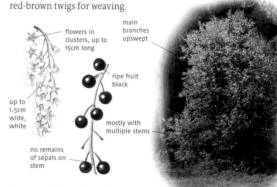

sparse form

main branches steeply ascending

often with multiple stems

leaf 5–12cm long, elongated oval

above leathery and rough, glossy, varnish-like

2 glands on leaf stalk

clusters of around 30 flowers

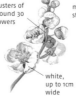

white, up to 1cm wide

Cherry Plum

Prunus cerasifera (rose family)

H 4–8m March–April

Gardeners like using the undemanding Cherry Plum as a rootstock for cultivating some sensitive varieties of Plum and Cherry. However, sometimes the rootstock produces shoots again later and can become stronger than the variety grafted onto it. The red-leafed tree is better known than the green-leafed wild tree with white blossom. These popular cultivars form red-brown leaves and pinkish flowers.

Habitat Native to Asia Minor and the Caucasus, naturalised in Europe, found in gardens and parks. Abundant flowers just before foliation.

> also known as the 'Mirabelle'
> flowers pink or white
> fruit colour varies from yellow to red

Did you know?

The fruits have an aromatic, generally slightly sour taste. The fruit flesh does not come away from the stone, unlike that of real plums (p. 106). It is therefore best to cook them whole with a little water and press the purée through a sieve.

leaf up to 7cm long, elliptic to oval

sparse hairs on veins below

fruit up to 3cm thick, spherical

crown squarrose, usually dense

103

generally with several stems

St. Lucie Cherry
Prunus mahaleb (rose family)
H 1–10m April–May

Habitat *Wild on sunny, stony slopes in central and southern Europe. Flowers like umbels.*

> also known as the 'Mahaleb Cherry'
> not sensitive to heat
> birds find sanctuary in the dense tree

flowers around 1.5cm in size, white

This trees tiny 'cherries' have a tart and usually bitter flavour. But this undemanding tree has still achieved a degree of importance: it is often used as a rootstock to cultivate different varieties of cherry. Its wood has a very pleasant scent, reminiscent of hay. It is excellent for woodturning work, such as making pipe stems.

6–10 together

crown broad, round

often found in different stages of maturity next to each other

fruits 6–8mm in size

leaf 3–8cm long, oval or round

bare and glossy above

crenate margin

branches squarrose

usually multiple stems, often shrub-like

Apricot
Prunus armeniaca (rose family)
H 4–8m March–April

Habitat *Native to western Asia. Common around the Mediterranean, rarely planted in central Europe. White or pink flowers appear before foliation.*

> 'Moorpark' most popular variety in Britain
> needs plenty of warmth
> fruit flesh comes away easily from the stone

Despite the species name *armeniaca*, the tree does not come from Armenia. However, it was brought to Greece and Rome following Roman emperor Nero's campaigns in Armenia in the first century AD. The fruits are very healthy to eat, containing a wealth of minerals and vitamins.

main branches often almost horizontal

crown rounded, often broadly spreading in cultivars

fruit 4–8cm in size, spherical to oval

leaf 5–10cm long

stem up to 7cm long, dark red

characteristic seam

one or more stems

pointed tip

Peach

Prunus persica (rose family)

H 3–10m   March–April

The species name *persica* stands as a reminder that the Peach came to Europe from its far-off home in China via Persia. The fruits have a refreshing taste and are highly aromatic. The kernels are poisonous since they may release prussic acid in the stomach. However, they supply a fatty oil, which is used in cosmetics, as is almond oil. Once the poisonous substances have been removed, the kernels can also be turned into persipan, a marzipan-like foodstuff.

Habitat Native to China. Frequently planted around the Mediterranean, only in areas with a wine-growing climate in central Europe. Fruits have characteristic velvety hairs.

> yellow and white-fleshed varieties
> easily digestible fruit
> flowers threatened by late frosts

Did you know?

The nectarine is a variety of peach with a smooth, hairless skin. It has been grown in Britain since the 16th century and there are now a wide range of different varieties on offer.

leaf 8–15cm long, broad and lanceolate

margin sharply serrated

crown spreading, rounded or flat

5 deep pink petals

flowers 1–3cm wide

one or more stems

kernel deeply grooved

fruit 5–7cm in size

Wild Plum

Prunus domestica (rose family)
H 3–15m   April–May

Habitat *Cultivated as a fruit tree throughout Europe, occasionally in the wild. Fruits often covered in a waxy bloom, which can be rubbed off.*

> *undemanding*
> *flowers just before or at the same time as foliation*
> *more than 2,000 varieties with very different fruits*

Archaeologists have found stones from different varieties of Wild Plum in prehistoric settlements in Europe and western Asia. The first cultivated plums came to Greece from Syria. The Romans then brought them to central Europe on their campaigns around 100 BC. The tasty fruits are excellent eaten raw, as a cake topping and in liqueurs. Both fresh and dried, they are good for the digestive system and are slightly laxative.

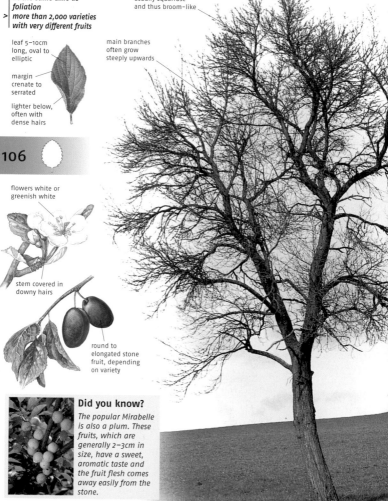

usually squarrose and thus broom-like

main branches often grow steeply upwards

leaf 5–10cm long, oval to elliptic

margin crenate to serrated

lighter below, often with dense hairs

flowers white or greenish white

stem covered in downy hairs

round to elongated stone fruit, depending on variety

Did you know?

The popular Mirabelle is also a plum. These fruits, which are generally 2–3cm in size, have a sweet, aromatic taste and the fruit flesh comes away easily from the stone.

Almond

Prunus dulcis (rose family)
H 3–10m   March–April

Almonds are highly nutritious and rich in key minerals. It would be hard to imagine Christmas without them. Many recipes require sweet almonds or marzipan, which is an aromatic paste consisting of ground almonds, sugar and flavouring. Almond oil is good for soothing baby skin and is used in natural cosmetics, as well as to oil timepieces. Bitter almonds, however, release prussic acid in the stomach. Five to ten Bitter Almond seeds can be fatal for children.

Habitat *Native to western Asia. Grown in the Mediterranean area. Flowers appear before leaves.*

> only thrives in highly protected areas of central Europe
> sensitive to late frost
> both sweet and bitter almonds exist

Did you know?

In the Mediterranean, green almonds with soft shells are considered a delicacy. When eaten raw, they taste best with a little salt or preserved in salt water.

some glands at base and on stem

leaf 8–12cm long, elongated and lanceolate or slender and oval

107

crown round to broadly spreading

flowers usually in pairs

3–5cm in size, pale pink or white

felt-like hairs

one or more stems

fruit flat and oval, 3–6cm long

dry fruit flesh

seeds are almonds

kernel very hard

Cockspur Hawthorn
Crataegus crus-galli (rose family)
H 6–10m May–June

Habitat *Native to eastern North America. Planted particularly as a roadside tree in Europe. Many flowers together of up to 1.5cm in size.*

> *undemanding*
> *foliage bright orange in autumn*
> *usually cultivated with a tall trunk, more rarely as a shrub*

crown elongated to round

branches splayed out

often appears somewhat squarrose

slender thorns up to 8cm long

often slightly curved

leathery feel

leaf 2–8cm long, oval

The Cockspur Hawthorn gets its name from the long thorns, which can make the tree form an impenetrable thicket. Cultivated with a tall trunk, the tree catches the eye by roadsides in spring with its rich display of flowers and in autumn with its beautifully coloured foliage, which remains on the twigs for a long time.

Japanese Flowering Crabapple
Malus floribunda (rose family)
H 3–10m May

fruits spherical, around 8mm in size

Habitat *Native to Japan. Ornamental tree in parks and gardens and by roadsides in Europe. Twigs often covered in dense blossoms.*

> *tolerates air pollution*
> *fruits extremely sour*
> *often used as a base species for cultivars*

The Japanese have been cultivating different varieties of this tree for many years. The richly blossoming tree first came to Europe in the 19th century, but quickly gained great popularity. With its mass of flowers, combined with an undemanding character, the tree is one of the most valuable ornamental apples.

crown broad, generally very dense

twigs often overhanging

older trees often gnarled

open flowers pink initially, soon paler

margin sharply serrated

grey-green below

leaf 3–8cm long, elliptic

flower buds red

Apple

Malus domestica (rose family)

H 2–15m   April–May

dried remains of
sepals on tip

Apple trees were cultivated by ancient
civilisations. During the reign of
Charlemagne, farmers cultivated several
different varieties of Apple. Today, there are
more than 2,000 varieties in Britain alone, but
only around 30 are grown commercially. The highly nutritious
fruits contain acids, sugar, pectin, vitamins and minerals.
There are far more vitamins in the peel than in the fruit flesh.

fruit rounded to
elongated, depending
on variety

Habitat Cultivated
tree, occasionally wild
in copses and on edges
of forests. Apples on
twigs on very short
stalks.

> *flowers at the same time
as foliation*
> *one of the most
important species of fruit*
> *around 20,000 known
varieties worldwide*

Did you know?

*Mixed orchards contain a variety of
fruit trees with tall trunks and are
usually cultivated near villages. This
traditional farming method provides
a habitat for many rare plants and
animals.*

serrated
margin

soft
hairs
below

leaf up to 12cm long,
broadly oval

5 white petals, often with a reddish tint

flowers up to 5cm wide

anthers yellow

form highly
variable

109

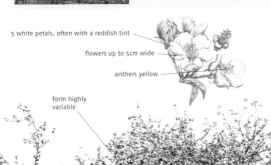

usually a
few very
strong
branches

Common Pear
Pyrus communis (rose family)
H 1–25m   April–May

leaf often has orange-red patches

Habitat *Only found in cultivation. Grown as a fruit tree throughout Europe. Leaves bright yellow to red in autumn.*

> *growth and form is very variable, depending on the variety and cut*
> *fruits ripen between July and October*
> *cultivated by ancient civilisations*

Pear trees with foliage can often be identified easily, even without their fruit. In summer and autumn, their leaves frequently have bright orange-red specks on the top and protruding pustules below. These leaves are infested with a rust fungus, which attacks pears and various species of juniper (p. 160) in turn. It does not appear on other trees.

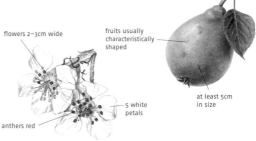

flowers 2–3cm wide

fruits usually characteristically shaped

at least 5cm in size

leaf 4–8cm long, rounded to oval

margin finely crenate

5 white petals

anthers red

crown usually higher than it is wide

distinctive main trunk or some strong upright branches

crown often slender to broadly conical or domed

Did you know?

The red-brown wood is extremely hard, heavy and durable. It can be polished to a beautiful sheen for furniture. The wood from the Wild Pear (see opposite page) is dyed black and used as a substitute for ebony.

Wild Pear

Pyrus pyraster (rose family)

H 5–20m April–May

The Wild Pear is regarded as an ancestor of the Common Pear. It differs from this in terms of its thorny twigs in particular. Wild red deer enjoy the ripe fruits, which lie on the ground as windfalls. In the Middle Ages, the fruits were fed to pigs. However, they are not fit for human consumption since they are tart and bitter.

conic crown

branches projecting to upswept

anthers red

3–9 flowers form an umbel

twigs often end in a thorn

straight trunk

Habitat *Native from Europe to western Asia in forests and rocky copses. Round to pear-shaped fruits only grow to 2–4cm across.*

> deep roots
> **needs sufficient warmth**
> **bark comprises small, square plates**

leaf stalk up to 7cm long

leaf 2–7cm long, rounded to oval

Whitebeam

Sorbus aria (rose family)

H 5–12m May–June

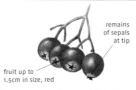

remains of sepals at tip

fruit up to 1.5cm in size, red

The felt-like hair on the leaves reduces evaporation, enabling the tree to grow in dry locations. The soft, floury, bland-tasting fruits can be eaten, but are only suitable as emergency sustenance. In the past, people dried and ground them and mixed them with flour to bake bread. They can also be used to produce vinegar.

crown oval to rounded

Habitat *Wild in central and western Europe in forests, dry copses and amongst rocks. Fruits often slightly hairy.*

> grows slowly
> **often planted along avenues or streets**
> **yellow-fruiting variety exists**

form usually fairly even

young leaves hairy above, later bare and shiny

flowers up to 1.5cm in size

many flowers in broad florets

leaf up to 10cm long, broadly oval

silvery white hairs below

Medlar

Mespilus germanica (rose family)
H 3–6m May–June

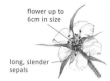

flower up to 6cm in size

long, slender sepals

Habitat Originated in western Asia. Around the Mediterranean since ancient times, brought to central Europe by the Romans. Fruits have distinctive remains of sepals.

> only rarely cultivated today
> fruits barely fit to be eaten raw
> beautiful ornamental tree

In the Middle Ages, the Medlar was a commonly eaten species of fruit, which Charlemagne expressly ordered to be grown. The fruits have a bitter, astringent taste and are only acceptable when they become soft and doughy with a musty scent. They improve the life span of apple and pear must when added to it.

spreading crown

leaf up to 15cm long and 3cm wide

grey-green below

margin finely serrated or even smooth

pointed tip

5 remaining sepal tips

fruit around 4cm wide

generally with several stems

indented top

112

Loquat

Eriobotrya japonica (rose family)
H 2–10m October–February

yellowish-white flowers with numerous stamens

Habitat Native to east Asia. Fruit tree in the Mediterranean and southern Alps. Flowers in dense, woolly florets.

> fairly hardy, even in central Europe
> unusual flowering season

Also known as the 'Japanese Medlar', the Loquat has a very pleasant, aromatic and sweet flavour when fully ripe. However, unripe fruits have a sour, often slightly astringent taste. The plant has woolly-haired new shoots and flowers.

several upswept main branches

fruit plum-sized

1–4 seeds

woolly and felted below

shiny above

leaf 15–20cm long, broad and lanceolate

toothed margin

evergreen leaves

Sweet Orange
Citrus sinensis (rue family)
H 5–8m April–October

The Sweet Orange was introduced to the Mediterranean far later than the Lemon, which was already known there in ancient times. Cultivation began in the 16th century. The tree's fruit can be eaten immediately and squeezed to produce juice. The peel and flower buds can be used to produce scented oil as a raw ingredient of perfume. Orange liqueur and other spirits are also flavoured with orange peel extracts, although sometimes from the Japanese Bitter Orange or Bitter Orange.

relatively spherical

some varieties have 'navel' or protuberance

fruit mostly
8–12cm in size

Habitat *Native to China. Cultivated as a fruit tree in southern Europe, as a pot plant in central Europe. Flowers pure white, unlike those of the Lemon.*

> *flowers have a strong, sweet scent*
> *ripeness of fruit differs depending on variety*
> *occasionally has thorns on twigs*

margin slightly crenate

leaf oval and elongated, dark green

stem with slender wings

113

Did you know?
The flesh of blood oranges contains red dyes. However, the fruits only produce these if the nights are cool. If the same varieties grow in the Tropics, the fruits remain orange.

evergreen tree

Lemon
Citrus limon (rue family)
H 2–7m January–December

Habitat Native to south-east Asia. Cultivated in the Mediterranean, as a pot plant in central Europe. Generally produces abundant fruit.

> blossoms and bears fruit all year round
> citric acid gives fruit juice a sour taste
> twigs with thorns

unevenly branched

sparse form

evergreen

Lemon juice is rich in vitamin C. By taking lemons on board ship, sailors were able to prevent scurvy, a disease caused by a vitamin C deficiency. For many years, lemons were a symbol of vitality and were used to ward off all evil, including the plague.

leaf 5–10cm long, light green

crenate margin

stalk with slender wings, if at all

25–40 stamens

5 petals

flower buds pink

114

Common Buckthorn
Rhamnus cathartica (buckthorn family)
H 2–6m May–June

stone fruits pea-sized, black when ripe

Habitat Wild through-out most of Europe in sunny hedgerows and on edges of forests. Fruits standing in dense clusters.

> male and female trees
> leaves opposite unlike those of the Alder Buckthorn (p. 70)
> poisonous!

Green paint can be made from the almost ripe fruits of the Common Buckthorn. This was once used by artists, as well as to dye paper and leather. The colour is known as 'sap green' or 'bladder green' because it was collected as a thick liquid in pig, cow or calf bladders and then dried in them.

form rounded, squarrose

strong branches

leaf oval to elliptic

3–4 curved side veins

margin finely serrated

flowers 4–5mm wide

4 greenish-yellow sepals

one or more short stems

English Holly

Ilex aquifolium (holly family)

H 2–8m May–June

In some areas, believers still carry holly twigs to church on Palm Sunday to have them sanctified. At Christmas, sprigs of holly make popular evergreen decorations, particularly in Britain. They symbolise the continuation of life during winter. All parts of the tree are poisonous. Twenty or 30 fruits would be enough to kill an adult.

4 white petals

male flower with 4 stamens

Habitat *Wild in forests from western Europe to Germany, in the Mediterranean. In gardens and parks. Fruits often remain on twigs in winter.*

> **leaves extremely spiky**
> **grows as a tree or shrub**
> **male and female plants**

slender form

curved stamens

female flower with 1 ovary

leaf up to 10cm long, rough and leathery, evergreen

margin wavy, usually with very spiky teeth

115

stone fruit up to 1cm in size, red

often smooth leaves along with the toothed

densely branched

Did you know?

There are many different varieties for gardens. Trees with variegated leaves are particularly popular, such as those with light edges or patches.

Small-leaved Lime

Tilia cordata (lime family)
H 10–30m   June–July

Many place names in Germany are associated with lime trees (known there as the 'Linde'), such as Lindau on Lake Constance and Leipzig. Lime leaves, together with the bract, produce a good, sweat-inducing tea to treat colds. The wood is soft and evenly structured so it can be worked easily and is one of the most popular types of wood among woodcarvers. Some of the most famous lime wood carvings include altars by Tilman Riemenschneider.

Habitat In forests of central and eastern Europe. In parks and streets throughout Europe. Eye-catching bracts between the leaves.

> *flowers have a strong scent and attract bees*
> *blossoms around 14 days later than the Large-leaved Lime*
> *sensitive to de-icing salt*

leaf 2–10cm long, heart-shaped

often slightly asymmetrical

rust-coloured hairs at axils below

116

old trunks often gnarled with thick growths

crown conical when young, later elongated to rounded

mostly 4–12 flowers together

flower stem merged with light-coloured bract

trunk fairly straight

Did you know?

The inner bark or bast has been well-known as a braiding and binding material for years. The 5,300 year-old mummy 'Ötzi', who was found in a glacier, wore shoes with inside braiding made of bast and a cloak into which lime bast was also worked.

Large-leaved Lime

Tilia platyphyllos (lime family)

H 15–40m   June

The lime played an important role in popular Germanic belief and was sanctified to the goddess of marriage and the hearth (Frigga). In the Middle Ages, village lime trees were at the centre of public life. People danced and celebrated beneath them. Limes also marked the spot where judicial rulings were made. Preservationists now put great effort into conserving these old and historical trees for as long as possible.

Habitat *Wild in central and southern Europe. Frequently planted in parks, streets and squares. Few fruits hanging from light bracts.*

> *leaves softer than those of the Small-leaved Lime*
> *needs plenty of humidity*
> *beautiful, particularly as a single tree*

Did you know?

Naturalists do not determine the seasons according to the calendar, but by the specific appearance of plants and animals. They regard the flowering of the Large-leaved Lime as a sign that midsummer is beginning.

flower stem merged with light-coloured bract

mostly 2–5 flowers together

leaf 5–16cm long, lopsided heart-shaped

whitish hairs at axils below

117

form mostly dense

crown broadly conical to round

Silver Lime

Tilia tomentosa (lime family)

H 10–30m   July

Bees can often be found swarming around beneath flowering Silver Limes. The nectar from this lime tree contains the sugar mannose, which bees and bumblebees cannot break down and can therefore be fatal to these insects. However, another reason could be that the insects can barely find any other food during the late flowering season of the Silver Lime and there is simply not enough nectar for all the visitors. Lime fruits are torn off by the wind, along with the bract, and twist in the air like little spinning tops.

Habitat *Native to south-west Europe. In parks and streets throughout Europe. Light underside of leaves characteristic.*

> *even grows well in streets with tarred surfaces*
> *tolerates exhaust fumes and smoke*
> *also as a pendulous form*

Did you know?

While other limes often cover cars parked below them with dirty, sticky droplets, vehicles beneath Silver Limes remain cleaner: because of all the hairs on the tree, there are far fewer aphids and it is their honeydew that produces the droplets.

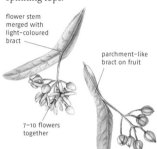

leaf up to 15cm long, heart-shaped, generally slightly asymmetrical

dark green above

silvery grey hairs below

flower stem merged with light-coloured bract

parchment-like bract on fruit

7–10 flowers together

fruits up to 1cm long

crown dense, broadly conical to round

main branches ascending

Dove Tree

Davidia involucrata (sour gum family)
H 15–20m May–June

head-like flower

2 differently sized bracts up to 16cm long

The white bracts move in the wind and are reminiscent of a fluttering flock of white doves or handkerchiefs hanging in the branches. The scientific name *Davidia* comes from the French missionary Armand David who discovered the tree in China in the 19th century.

branches upswept or horizontal

form broadly conical

Habitat Native to China. In parks and botanical collections in Europe. Flowers appear at the same time as foliage.

> needs mild winters
> flowers for around two weeks
> also known as the 'Handkerchief Tree'

stem thickened

stem red

fruit up to 3.5cm in size

ripe fruit light to violet-brown

leaf up to 15cm long, heart-shaped

long tip

long leaf stalk

Strawberry Tree

Arbutus unedo (heather family)
H 1.5–10m October–March

flower around 9mm in size

bell-shaped with 5 tips

form tree or shrub-like, dense

Although the fruits slightly resemble strawberries, the Strawberry Tree is not related to them and does not share their aroma. Unripe fruits are floury and merit the species name *unedo*, meaning 'I eat only one'. Ripe fruits are juicy and sweet and sour. The Portuguese distil Medronho from the fermented fruits – a brandy containing around 40 per cent alcohol.

Habitat In the Mediterranean in evergreen forests and shrubland areas. By the Atlantic as far as Ireland. Flowers eye-catching in winter.

> also known as the 'Cane Apple'
> often grows together with the Tree Heath (p. 58)
> tolerates shade well

evergreen foliage

fruit 1.5–2cm in size, ripens as of September

yellow initially, later red

warty

leaf leathery, shiny

margin finely serrated

4–11cm long

White Poplar
Populus alba (willow family)
H 15–30m   March–April

Habitat *Wild in central and southern Europe in riverside forests. Planted in gravel pits, by roadsides. Bark whitish, often with diamond-shaped fissures.*

> *bright silvery white from a distance, particularly in windy weather*
> *tolerates aridity*
> *resistant to factory fumes*

The White Poplar requires far less water than the Black Poplar (p. 85). It grows on roadside embankments or spoil heaps, often just as a shrub, and is good for stabilising the ground with its extensive, shallow root system. Whole groups of young trees frequently grow around the original tree.

underside of leaf and stem white to grey, felted

Did you know?

According to legend, the eye-catching white underside of the leaves was created by the sweat of Hercules. He crowned himself with a wreath of White Poplar when he brought Cerberus, the Hound of Hades, out of the Underworld.

leaf 4–12cm long, 3–5 lobes

dark green above

blunt teeth on margin

120

crown broadly oval or rounded

male flower with crimson anthers

catkins up to 8cm long, shaggy hairs

female catkins with yellow stigmas

often with off-shoots at base

Turkey Oak

Quercus cerris (beech family)

H 20–30m April

The Turkey Oak thrives in dry spots with few nutrients and is resistant to fumes. It is therefore being planted more and more often along busy roads as well as in parks. Its hard wood makes excellent fuel, but can also be used in construction.

Habitat Wild in the south of central Europe and southern Europe. Planted in parks and along roads. Fruit cups with dense scales unmistakable.

crown broadly conical to rounded

branches projecting and squarrose

> *felt-like hairs on underside of leaves*
> *form resembles that of the English Oak (p. 122)*
> *acorns ripen in 2nd year*

acorn up to 2.5cm long

fruit cup with pointed, projecting scales up to 1cm long

leaf 6–11cm long

4–9 mostly pointed lobes on each side

Red Oak

Quercus rubra (beech family)

H 10–25m May

Mushroom gatherers generally find plenty in oak forests. But planted Red Oak forests are hardly worth a visit as few mushrooms live near this oak. The tree has very deep roots and can be grown on the edges of forests to protect them from storms.

Habitat Native to eastern North America. In forests and parks of central Europe. Scarlet to bright orange in autumn.

branches broadly spreading

crown conical initially, later rounded

straight trunk, usually reaches up to tree top

> *needs plenty of light*
> *grows rapidly when young*
> *acorns ripen in 2nd year*

acorn rounded to oval

stem short, thick

fruit cup flat

leaf 10–25cm long

2–6 angular, pointed lobes on each side

English Oak

Quercus robur (beech family)
H 20–35m   April–May

Habitat In forests throughout most of Europe. One of the most important forest trees in central Europe. Outer woody area light, inner darker.

> probably the best-known tree in Britain
> life span up to 1,000 years
> fresh English Oak wood smells sour

The English Oak was highly revered in the past. The Germanic tribes consecrated it to Donar, the god of thunder, and it was the holiest tree of the Celts. In Christianity, it was also considered holy and was popularly planted at sites of pilgrimage. The tree symbolises strength, power, peace and growth. In Britain, the English Oak population was decimated in the 17th and 18th centuries, owing to the huge demand for timber for shipbuilding and construction work.

female flowers have long stems

male flowers form hanging catkins

1/4–1/3 enclosed in a fruit cup

acorn up to 3.5cm long

1–5 fruits on long stalk

leaf 7–15cm long, short stemmed

5–7 mostly blunt lobes on each side

small ears at base

form broad, rather uneven

branches strong, broadly spreading, often gnarled, twisted and crooked

Did you know?

Oak leaves frequently have strange patterns on them. These galls are caused by various insects, with one or more larvae living in each one. Scientists can identify more than 100 types of gall on oaks.

Sessile Oak

Quercus petraea (beech family)
H 20–30m   April–May

1/4 enclosed in a fruit cup
almost no stem
acorn up to 3cm long

The firm, hard wood of the Sessile Oak (and the English Oak) is almost fully resistant to damp and has supplied durable piles for building foundations for centuries. Some historical buildings and old towns, such as in Venice and Amsterdam, stand largely on oak logs. Railway sleepers were also manufactured from these woods for many years.

crown high-domed

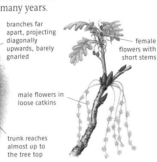

branches far apart, projecting diagonally upwards, barely gnarled

female flowers with short stems

male flowers in loose catkins

trunk reaches almost up to the tree top

Habitat *Wild from central Europe to Asia Minor, particularly on plains and hills. Frequently in forests. Foliage yellow–brown in autumn.*

> *flowers around two weeks later than the English Oak*
> *dry autumn foliage often remains on the tree for a long time*
> *sensitive to waterlogging*

stem 1–1.5cm long, yellow
leaf 8–12cm long

4–9 blunt, even lobes on both sides

123

Downy Oak

Quercus pubescens (beech family)
H 5–10m   April–May

After the last Ice Age, the Downy Oak was widespread and formed forests in central Europe. Over time, however, it was ousted by other trees, particularly the Common Beech (p. 60). It can still be found today in a few very warm places, such as the Kaiserstuhl, southern Baden or Saaletal near Jena in Germany.

crown fairly broad

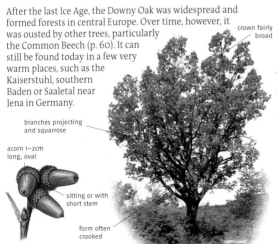

branches projecting and squarrose

acorn 1–2cm long, oval

sitting or with short stem

form often crooked

Habitat *Especially in southern Europe in dry, warm forests. Leaves clearly felted on underside.*

> *sometimes grows as a shrub*
> *forms large forests, particularly in southern France*
> *needs warmth*

4–8 rounded lobes on each side
leaf 7–10cm long

light grey-green below, felted

Fig Tree
Ficus carica (mulberry family)
H 3–10m June–September

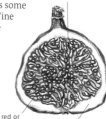

contains small, hard nutlets

red or green flesh

ripe figs 5–8cm long

Habitat *Widely cultivated across southern Europe, some also growing wild. Figs are on short stalks in leaf axils.*

> *shoots emerge in late spring*
> *contains milky sap*
> *often in shelter of walls and houses*

Fig trees were first planted by the Assyrians some 5,000 years ago. Together with the Grape Vine (p. 240) and Olive Tree (p. 79), the Fig is one of the oldest cultivated trees. Throughout history it has been cultivated right across the Mediterranean. Figs are not true fruits but so-called false fruits: the actual fruits are the tiny hard nutlets that crunch when you eat them and are enclosed within.

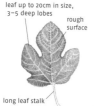

leaf up to 20cm in size, 3–5 deep lobes

rough surface

long leaf stalk

124

loose foliage

thick, grey twigs

sparse form

with single or multiple stems

Did you know?
Dried figs are healthy as well as tasty. As well as sugar they contain substantial amounts of calcium, potassium and iron, which stimulate the body's production of blood cells. They are also effective as a mild laxative for constipation.

White Mulberry

Morus alba (mulberry family)

H 6–15m May–June

White Mulberry leaves are the main food source for silkmoth larvae. The larvae pupate into a cocoon made up of one single thread of silk, which can reach up to 3,500 metres in length. The Chinese have been breeding silkworms on the White Mulberry for over 3,000 years. They brought the product to Europe via the Silk Road. Silkmoth eggs came to Europe in the 6th century, making European silk production possible. However, intensive silk production only commenced from the 16th century onwards.

Habitat *Originates from China. Cultivated in warm European countries and partly growing wild. Found in parks of central Europe. Fruit ripens in June.*

> *bland-tasting fruit*
> *also suitable for hedgerows*
> *also as hanging variety with ripe black fruits*

Did you know?
Very old white mulberry trees can be found in many French villages. Some of these at least were planted to create an additional source of income from the valuable silk.

inconspicuous, greenish female flowers

in long flower clusters up to 2cm long

leaf up to 20cm long, often 3–5-lobed

sparse hairs, if any

125

variable leaves, unlobed

blackberry-like fruit, up to 3cm long

mainly white to pink

dense, circular crown

single trunk, mainly short, sometimes also with multiple stems

Paper Mulberry
Broussenetia papyrifera (mulberry family)
H 3–6m May–June

Habitat *Native to China and Japan. Grown as ornamental trees in southern Europe, some also grow wild. Female flowers form spherical heads.*

> **contains milky sap**
> **both male and female trees exist**
> **requires warm summers and mild winters**

In the first century AD the Chinese manufactured the first paper from the bark of the Paper Mulberry. They crushed the bark into a fibrous paste and passed it through a bamboo sieve. By drying, smoothing out and then treating the paste with glue, they managed to produce thin, durable sheets. Nowadays genuine mulberry paper can only be found occasionally in art and craft shops.

fruit stalks about 2cm wide

wide-spreading crown

fruit club-shaped, orange when ripe

rough, hairy surface

leaf up to 20cm long, 3-lobed or oval

with short single stem or multiple stems

Ague Tree
Sassafras albidum (laurel family)
H 10–18m April–May

Habitat *Native to the north-eastern part of North America. Grown in parks of Europe.*

> **Inconspicuous flowers appear together with leaves.**
> **parts smell aromatic when crushed**
> **autumn foliage yellow or red**

The North American Indians used the wood and bark from the aromatic roots of this tree as a substitute for tobacco and also to give drinks an aroma. In Europe the roots and the oil extracted from them were used as an effective diuretic. Nowadays it is regarded as unsafe, as some elements are known to cause cancer.

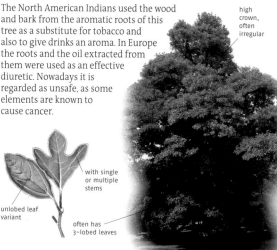

high crown, often irregular

with single or multiple stems

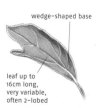

wedge-shaped base

leaf up to 16cm long, very variable, often 2-lobed

unlobed leaf variant

often has 3-lobed leaves

Tulip Tree

Liriodendron tulipfera (magnolia family)

H 20–30m May–June

The Tulip Tree is regarded as one of the most important trees in North American forestry. It produces a light timber, which is easy to work with and has a glossy finish. The timber industry uses it by the name of 'Whitewood' or 'Yellow Poplar' for boats, furniture and interior extensions. Wherever the Tulip Tree grew some 200 years ago, nearly every log cabin was made out of its wood.

many winged fruit

aggregate, cone-like fruit, 6–8 cm in size

Habitat Originates from the eastern part of North America. Grown in parks of Europe. Striking flowers resembling tulips.

> **strong golden-yellow autumn colours**
> **distinctive leaves**
> **can reach an age of up to 700 years**

6 petals, about 5cm long

abundant stamens

many ovaries

mainly 4 pointed lobes

loose crown, columnar to circular

leaf up to 25cm long, almost square

127

thick branches, often gnarled

Did you know?

Liriodendron translates as 'Lily Tree' or 'Narcissus Tree'. The botanist Linnaeus gave the tree this name in the 18th century, on comparing its large, single flowers to those of the lily and narcissus or daffodil.

London Plane
Platanus x *hispanica* (plane family)
H 10–35m May

Habitat *Not known to grow in the wild. Probably a European hybrid between the American and Oriental Plane. Common along streets and in parks. Large, thin pieces of wood flake off the bark.*

> **alternate leaves, unlike the Maple**
> **tolerates polluted atmospheres**
> **rapid growth**

leaf up to 20cm long, 3–7 triangular lobes

stalk thickens at base

Plane trees can live up to 400 years on sufficiently moist soils, though they can also tolerate dry soils and urban atmospheres. Urban trees often fall victim, however, to a fungus which penetrates the tree via scars on the branches and, in doing so, kills off parts of the crown or indeed the entire tree. In urban areas many plane trees are felled for safety reasons if their thick branches become too brittle.

male flowers green and spherical

female flowers red and spherical

up to 2–3 on long stalks

round, spiny fruit stems, up to 4 cm across

often remaining on tree over winter

large, wide-spreading crown

trunk often with several parts

thick branches, lower ones overhanging

Did you know?
Plane trees can be cut well back and can therefore be pruned as desired for avenues and streets. Severely stunted specimens can be seen particularly in southern European towns.

Sweet Gum Tree

Liquidambar styraciflua (witch-hazel family)
H 10–25m May

crown spherical at first, oval later on

The furniture industry has only taken a serious interest in the hard, heavy, reddish-brown timber produced by the Sweet Gum Tree over the last 100 years. The so-called 'Satinwood' is a good substitute for Walnut and is widely used for furniture manufacture. When damaged, the bark releases a pleasant-smelling resin called 'Styrax', which was previously used in chewing-gum.

Habitat *Native to south-eastern areas of the United States. In parks in Europe, gardens, on roadsides. In autumn, leaves turn deep red, orange or yellow.*

> **alternate leaves**
> **camphor odour when crushed**
> **fruit often remains on tree over winter**

main branches relatively horizontal

trunk straight up into apex

flower clusters spherical

spiky, woody

multiple fruits up to 3.5cm in size

leaf up to 20cm wide, 5–7 pointed lobes

fine serrated margin

129

Midland Hawthorn

Crataegus laevigata 'Paul's Scarlet' (rose family)
H 2–8m May–June

irregular circular crown

The Midland Hawthorn came into being in the 19th century as a strain of the Hawthorn (p. 221). Because of its small crown and abundant blossom, it soon became a popular urban tree. However, it forms numerous wild shoots on its trunk, which must be removed at regular intervals. It is also susceptible to greenfly.

Habitat *Only familiar as a cultivated tree. A roadside tree in particular, less common in parks and gardens. Especially distinctive because of its blossom.*

> **also known as 'Paul's Scarlet Hawthorn'**
> **rarely produces fruit**
> **thorny branches**

usually with high trunk

often 5–10 flowers close together

brilliant crimson red, densely packed

leaf 3–5-lobed, up to 5cm long

lobes finely serrated

Wild Service Tree

Sorbus torminalis (rose family)
H 5–20m May–June

oval fruit, up to 2cm long

brown and flecked when ripe

Habitat *Grows in the wild on warm slopes in southern and central Europe. Planted on wood margins. Autumn foliage glows yellow, brownish-red or brilliant red.*

> **only as shrubs if found growing on rocks**
> **deep roots**
> **requires plenty of warmth**

This hard wood is one of the most expensive native woods. Also known as the 'Chequer Tree', it is used to produce precious reddish-brown veneers, rulers and measures. The fruit contains lots of tannin and tastes bitter. It was once used to counteract diarrhoea containing blood. *Torminalis* is derived from 'tormina', the Latin name for this complaint.

white flowers, about 1.5cm in size

crown oval to spherical with dense branches

loosely packed flower head, with downy hairs

with one or multiple stems

leaf up to 12cm long

on each side 3–4 broadly pointed, indented lobes

Vosges Whitebeam

Sorbus mougeotii (rose family)
H 8–20m June

Habitat *Grows in the wild in the mountainous regions of southern, central and western Europe. Red 1cm berries, a radiant contrast from autumn foliage.*

> **white, downy leaf underside**
> **growth pattern resembles Whitebeam (p. 111)**
> **requires plenty of sun**

This tree is very common in the Vosges mountains and is particularly distinctive in autumn. It is regarded as a naturally formed hybrid of the Whitebeam (p. 111) and the Mountain Ash or Rowan (p. 141). As with the Swedish Whitebeam, its fruit is edible when cooked but does not taste particularly good.

crown oval to spherical, fairly regular

branches pushing upwards

flower head slightly curved

white flowers, up to 1.2cm in size

often with multiple stems

leaf 7–10cm long, loosely lobed

8–12 pairs of leaf veins

Swedish Whitebeam

Sorbus intermedia (rose family)
H 12–15m May

Just like the Vosges Whitebeam, the Swedish Whitebeam is also considered to be a natural hybrid. It developed in parts of Scandinavia since the last Ice Age, seemingly from the Whitebeam (p. 111), the Mountain Ash or Rowan (p. 141) and Wild Service Tree (p. 130). Its seeds develop without pollination, thereby retaining the characteristics of the parent tree.

crown oval to circular, mainly regular

Habitat *Native to Scandinavia and around Baltic Sea. Also found in parks and on roadsides in central Europe. Foliage slightly reminiscent of oak leaves.*

> *leaf underside very grey and downy*
> *very undemanding and hardy*
> *widely planted*

fruit up to 15mm long, elongated, orangey-red, lightly mottled

main branches slanting upwards

short trunk

leaf up to 10cm long, coarsely lobed

7–9 pairs of leaf veins

131

Sycamore

Acer pseudoplatanus (maple family)
H 25–30m May

The Sycamore is among one of the most valuable native deciduous trees. The light, easily worked wood is used in the production of furniture and parquet flooring as well as kitchen utensils, such as steak hammers and wooden spoons. Musical instrument makers hold it in high regard for the production of woodwind instruments as well as sound boxes for stringed instruments.

wide crown, conical to circular

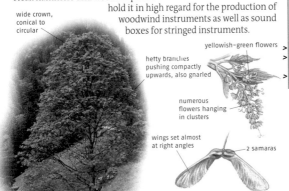

Habitat *Native to ravined or mountainous woods of central and southern Europe. Commonly found in parks and on roadsides. Ripe fruit often remaining on tree for some time.*

yellowish-green flowers

hetty branches pushing compactly upwards, also gnarled

numerous flowers hanging in clusters

wings set almost at right angles

2 samaras

> *opposite leaves*
> *blossom flowering at same time as leaves*
> *requires humidity and partial shade*

5-lobed leaf, up to 20cm long

irregular margin, coarsely serrated

Norway Maple
Acer platanoides (maple family)
H 15–25m April–May

Habitat Grows wild in forests of Europe, Asia Minor and the Caucasus. Planted in parks, gardens and on roadsides. Autumn leaves range from golden-yellow to red.

> opposite leaves
> flowers appearing before foliage, trees then with a yellow-green glow
> also as a dark-red garden variety

The words Acer and maple are both derived from the Indo-European word 'ak', which means 'sharp, pointed', due to the points on the margins of maple leaves. With the rise in sugar cane prices in Europe at the end of the 18th century, the sap from the Norway Maple was extracted, as it contains 3–4 per cent sugar. Although this experimentation promised success, in the end, the extraction of sugar from sugar beet actually won through.

Did you know?
Black spots are commonly found on the leaves of native maples. This is caused by infection with fungus that gives rise to 'Tar Spot' disease. The foliage does not look as attractive, but the disease is not damaging to the tree itself.

large pointed toothed margin

stalk containing milky sap

leaf 12–18cm long, mainly 5-lobed

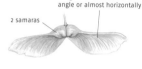

2 samaras

wings stick out at an obtuse angle or almost horizontally

flowers in upright clusters

flowers yellowish-green, about 1cm in size

crown circular to conical, wide-spreading, especially in aging tree

heavily forked branches

Field Maple

Acer campestre (maple family)
H 5–15m May–June

Children are prone to play around with maple seeds. After all, who as a child has not been tempted to bend back the winged seeds and stick them on their nose? The ripe fruit spins as it falls just like helicopters and, in doing so, increases its flight distance.

Habitat Grows in the wild, particularly in central Europe, in woodlands and copses out on open fields. Planted in gardens and parks. Trunks and twigs often with distinctive bark.

crown circular to conical, wide-spreading

densely branched

2 samaras

wings stick out almost horizontally

upright panicle with 10–12 yellow-green flowers

with one or multiple stems

> **leaves opposite**
> **dense shrub, often found in undergrowth**
> **also called 'Common Maple'**

leaf up to 8cm long, 3–5-lobed

rounded lobes

notched margin

133

Montpellier Maple

Acer monspessulanum (maple family)
H 5–11m April–May

According to Homer's 'Iliad', the Greeks constructed the Trojan Horse out of wood from the maple tree. Perhaps Montpellier Maple or Norway Maple was used. Both are found as far as Asia Minor. The fact that today the tree is found near castles on the rivers Rhine, Moselle and Main suggests that the tree was once planted in castle gardens.

Habitat Native to southern Europe and western Asia. Cultivated especially for hedgerows. Wings on circular fruit turn red in sunny locations.

> **opposite leaves**
> **often as a shrub**

crown broadly rounded-off or circular

branches stretching upwards

in overhanging clusters

flowers appearing at same time as leaves

topside of leaf rounded

smooth margin

leaf usually only up to 5cm long, 3-lobed, tough

Italian Maple
Acer opalus (maple family)
H 8–15m March–April

Habitat *Native to the mountainous forests of south-west Europe. Parks and gardens in central Europe.*

> **Fruit with pointed wings protruding at right angles.**
> **opposite leaves**
> **tolerates most types of soil**

leaf 6–10cm wide, rounded, tough, 3–5-lobed

crenate margin

dense crown, wide-spreading dome

The Italian Maple reaches the most northerly point of its natural distribution at the bend of the river Rhine in the south-western corner of Germany. It requires sufficient warmth, despite being undemanding in terms of soil quality. In favourable climates it can grow into an attractive ornamental tree.

yellow flowers hanging in clusters

with one or multiple stems

Japanese Maple
Acer palmatum (maple family)
H 2–4m May

Habitat *Originates from Japan and Korea. Popular decorative tree for gardens and parks. Many varieties with red-coloured leaves.*

> **opposite leaves**
> **very variable leaf types**
> **many cultivated varieties are shrub-like**

Varieties of the Japanese Maple are among the most popular of our garden trees. Gardeners like to plant, in particular, the different smaller varieties with deeply cut leaves and strange growth patterns in front gardens and grounds. When left to grow independently, these decorative trees develop into beautiful eye-catching specimens.

2 samaras

samara wings slightly angled inwards

dense crown, spread out umbrella-like

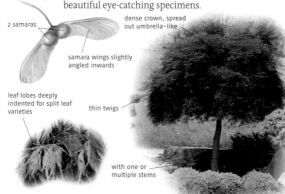

thin twigs

leaf up to 12cm long, 5–11-lobed

margin finely serrated

narrow lobes, long and pointed

leaf lobes deeply indented for split leaf varieties

with one or multiple stems

Silver Maple

Acer saccharinum (maple family)

H 15–20m March

The Silver Maple grows very rapidly and looks really attractive only a few years after being planted. This is why gardeners value it highly as a decorative tree. However, it can only live up to 125 years at the most and as it ages, becomes very brittle, which is why regular monitoring of the trees is carried out in public grounds. Compared to that of other maples, its wood is of poor quality as it is light and quite soft.

reddish-brown scales

Habitat *Originates from eastern United States of America. Commonly found in green areas, parks and gardens. When leaf shoots appear, young fruits are already formed*

> *opposite leaves*
> *fruit ripens in June*
> *tolerates polluted air*

female flower with red scars

flowers in dense clusters

wings forming a U- or V-shape

2 samaras

curved wings

leaf 7–14cm across, symmetrical, 5-lobed

underside white or pale grey

deeply indented as far as and beyond centre

lobes deeply serrated

domed crown

branches often over-hanging

mainly with multiple stems

Did you know?

Saccharinum *is derived from the Latin word 'saccharum' meaning 'sugar'. Sugar can be extracted from the spring sap, though the Silver Maple yields less than the Sugar Maple (p. 136).*

Sugar Maple
Acer saccharum (maple family)
H 10–15m April–May

Habitat Native to eastern North America. Occasionally in Europe as an ornamental tree. Leaves turn yellow and scarlet in autumn.

> opposite leaves
> underside of leaf light green or whitish
> maple leaf portrayed on Canada's national flag

n springtime, North American people collect the sap of the Sugar Maple by making a 5cm-deep incision in its bark. They then heat this sap, which is 5-7 per cent sugar, over log fires to make maple syrup or sugar. They then heat the sap over log fires to make Maple syrup or sugar. This is one of the healthiest sweetening agents, as it contains valuable minerals.

crown mainly irregular, increases with age

branches stretching upwards

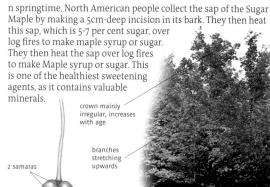

leaf 8–15cm across, 3–5-lobed, relatively thin

2 samaras

wings almost parallel or V-shaped

pointed toothed margin

Chinese Catalpa
Catalpa ovata (bignonia family)
H 3–15m July

Habitat Originates from western China. In gardens and parks of central and southern Europe. Distinctive in autumn due to its plentiful elongated fruits.

> intolerant of severe frosts
> fruit up to 40cm long and 8mm thick, resembles cigarillos
> leaves occasionally even unlobed

The Japanese frequently plant the Chinese Catalpa as an ornamental tree. In Europe, it is less common than the Indian Bean Tree (p.78). The Chinese Catalpa only grows in the wild in North America and Asia. During the tertiary period (up to two million years ago) several other varieties of Chinese Catalpa were also growing in Europe. However, during the Ice Ages, it became too cold for them and they died out.

rounded-off apex

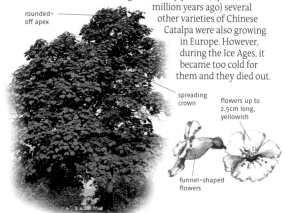

spreading crown

flowers up to 2.5cm long, yellowish

pointed

leaf up to 25cm long, mainly 3–5-lobed, firm

funnel-shaped flowers

Common Walnut

Juglans regia (walnut family)

H 15–25m May

The Romans brought the Common Walnut over to central Europe because of its many uses. Nowadays farmers plant it in preference to other trees because of its tasty seeds which are rich in oil. Old trees can be found growing around farms, as it used to be believed that they warded off flies and midges. Nothing much flourishes under this tree, which is not just because of its shade. Rather it is due to the fact that the tree contains substances which suppress the germination and growth of many other plants.

inconspicuous green female flowers

green stone fruit, up to 5cm

wrinkled nut

male flowers form drooping catkins

trunk mostly short

broad crown, circular to oval

Habitat Originated in Asia and the eastern Mediterranean. Planted in warmer regions of Europe. Green nut shells split open while still on the tree.

> often grows as a single tree
> yields beautiful timber for furniture
> numerous varieties with various large fruits

5–9 coarse, bare leaflets

odd-pinnate leaf, up to 40cm long

margin mostly smooth

137

wide-spreading branches

Did you know?

If the sap from fresh walnut leaves or the green nut shells comes into contact with the skin, it turns a strong yellowish-brown colour that lasts for a long time. Consequently some tinted sunscreen products contain a certain amount of walnut leaf extract.

Black Walnut

Juglans nigra (walnut family)
H 15–30m May

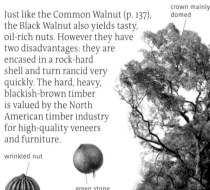

crown mainly domed

loose crown, irregular, wide-spreading

Habitat *Native to eastern United States of America. Planted as an ornamental tree in parks and estate grounds of Europe. Nuts within green fruit shells are hard to crack open.*

> green shell does not burst open independently
> only suitable for large parks

Just like the Common Walnut (p. 137), the Black Walnut also yields tasty, oil-rich nuts. However they have two disadvantages: they are encased in a rock-hard shell and turn rancid very quickly. The hard, heavy, blackish-brown timber is valued by the North American timber industry for high-quality veneers and furniture.

odd-pinnate leaf, up to 60cm long

15–23 leaflets

margin irregularly serrated

wrinkled nut

green stone fruit, up to 5cm in size

male catkins, 10–15cm long

Caucasian Wingnut

Pterocarya fraxinifolia (walnut family)
H 10–20m April–May

Habitat *Wild in the Caucasus as far as northern Iran. In parks of central Europe. Fruit makes this tree particularly distinctive.*

> very picturesque as free-standing tree
> young trees often produced from roots
> yellow autumn foliage

In its native habitat this tree grows in meadow woodlands alongside rivers. In Europe it also responds best to damp soil near ponds and streams, but it can withstand heat and urban environments. The timber is soft and difficult to split but has a lovely grain.

broad crown

up to 27 narrow, elongated leaflets

finely serrated margin

odd-pinnate leaf, up to 50cm long

fruit up to 2cm in width

2 semi-circular wings

fruit stalks up to 45cm long

branched usually as far as base

often with multiple stems

Shagbark Hickory

Carya ovata (walnut family)
H 20–25m May

This tree produces sweet-tasting 'hickory nuts' which are popular in the USA but are, however, less in demand than the closely related pecan nut (see box). The thin shells around the fruit are very easy to crack open and, on some varieties, they are paper-thin. The tree arouses interest from the forestry industry: hickory timber is both very hard and yet elastic. It is therefore ideal for making wheel spokes and sports equipment, for example.

4 lengthwise grooves

stone fruit up to 5cm long

shell opens up into 4 parts

light-coloured nut, circular or square

strong, towering main branches

wide-spreading

in old trees, crown often in several parts

Habitat Native to eastern parts of North America. Grows in parks of central and southern Europe. Bark cracked, peels off in shingle-like flakes.

> *leaves release fragrance when crushed*
> *golden-yellow autumn foliage*
> *requires warm climate in wine-growing areas*

pinnate leaf mainly with 5 leaflets

lower leaf pair much smaller

terminal leaflet up to 20cm

139

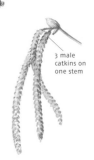

3 male catkins on one stem

Did you know?

The fruit of the closely related pecan nut (Carya illinoinensis) is considered a healthy and tasty food. In former times they were an important winter food source for the Indians. Astronauts of the Apollo flights were allowed to eat pecan nuts as their only source of fresh food.

Finnish Whitebeam

Sorbus x *hybrida* (rose family)
H 7–10m May–June

Habitat Native to southern parts of Scandinavia. In parks and on roadsides of central Europe. Flowers form stems up to 10cm wide.

> underside of leaves grey and downy
> fruit edible when cooked, mealy, somewhat sharp
> often cultivated as tall-stemmed tree

The characteristics of the Finnish Whitebeam lie halfway between those of the Whitebeam (p. 111) and those of the Rowan (p. 141). This can be seen especially clearly by its leaves. The tree was described in 1762 for the first time and was considered to be a hybrid of both the named varieties. Its pollen is unproductive but germinating seeds develop even without pollination.

crown slender initially, broad oval to circular later on

numerous branches

spherical fruit, up to 1.5cm in diameter

trunk usually short

red, slightly spotted

large, lobed top section

basal leaf with 1–3 pinnate pairs

140

True Service

Sorbus domestica (rose family)
H 10–20m May–June

fruit spherical or pear-shaped, up to 3cm

Habitat Wild in southern central Europe and in southern Europe. Cultivated and wild in winegrowing areas. Fruit resembles small apples or pears.

> used as a substitute for cider or perry
> considered to be one of the oldest fruit trees
> nowadays quite rare

If you have ever bitten into a seemingly ripe yet hard fruit from the True Service tree, you will never forget the experience: the tannic acid it contains has such a bitter taste that you are inclined to spit it straight out again. It leaves a fuzzy, almost numbing sensation in the mouth and a choking feeling in the throat.

crown roundish initially, irregular later on

branches often gnarled

trunk stretches as far as treetop

underside whitish-green, some hairs

odd-pinnate leaf with 11–21 leaflets

flowers form conical clusters

flowers about 1.5cm in size

Rowan

Sorbus aucuparia (rose family)
H 5–15m May–June

This tree is also known as the 'Mountain Ash'. Birds eat the fruits in winter, excreting undigested seeds and in doing so ensuring the seeds' dispersal. Even in the old days, bird catchers would lure their prey with the fruits. The Rowan was known in the Second World War as the 'Lemon of the North', as it is rich in vitamin C. The German name for this tree contains a reference to the 'boar' as it was once used for pig fodder.

Habitat Wild in woodlands all over Europe and on rocky outcrops. Commonly planted in parks and gardens. Conspicuous fruit attracts birds.

> **most attractive trees grow mainly in mountainous regions**
> **pleasant-smelling flowers**
> **fruit edible when cooked**

fruits up to 1cm in size, orangey-red

crown circular to oval, usually slightly squarrose

odd-pinnate leaf with 9–17 leaflets

serrated margin

underside grey to bluish-green

141

distinctive flower clusters, up to 15cm wide

flowers about 1cm in size

Did you know?

It is well worth planting the very similar 'Mountain Ash, Edulis' (Sorbus aucuparia 'edulis') as a fruit for stewing and spirits. Its fruit is less bitter to taste, rich in sugar and can be enjoyed raw.

one or multiple stems

Mimosa

Acacia dealbata (mimosa family)
H 4–15m January–April

Habitat Wild in
S.E. Australia and
Tasmania. Commonly
cultivated in the
Mediterranean. Small
flower heads form
prolific flower stalks.

> evergreen
> tolerates aridness
> flowering branches in
florists in late winter

The Mimosa and some other acacias are grown around the
Mediterranean for ornamental purposes, as wind-breakers and to
combat soil erosion. These trees can prosper on nutrient-deficient
soils. They have small nodules on their
roots which host certain bacteria that
absorb essential nitrogen from
the air. Australia is the home for
over half the 700 varieties of
acacias – this is why Australians
have chosen the acacia as their
national emblem.

yellow flower heads,
about 0.6cm in size

leaf bi-pinnate

glands at
base of the
pinnate
pairs

fruit 4–10cm long

flat, wavy

142

loose crown, often irregular

Did you know?

*Scale insects live off this tree. These creatures
deposit a resiny substance, from which shellac
is produced. This substance used to play a large
role in shellac record production. Nowadays
it is used in furniture restoration and as a
substitute for sugar frosting under the name
of E904.*

Pink Siris

Albizia julibrissin (mimosa family)
H 5–15m May–September

many pink or pale lilac stamens, up to 3cm long

flower clusters up to 5cm across

This tree is also known as the 'Silk Tree'. Indeed, the delicate, attractive flower bundles really do look as if they are made out of silk. The numerous thin stamens form the highly distinctive tufts. The small feathery leaflets can move on their own 'hinges' and at night they all point vertically downwards.

crown widely domed, sometimes almost umbrella-shaped

Habitat Indigenous to Persia and as far as central China. Widely spread in the Mediterranean as an ornamental tree. Flower clusters extend upwards.

> seeds germinant for a long time
> very suitable for arid, warm, southern locations

fruit up to 15cm long

light brown, flat, corrugated

leaf bi-pinnate

up to 30cm long

many small leaflets

Honey Locust

Gleditsia triacanthos (legume family)
H 15–20m June–July

greenish flowers in racemes, up to 8cm long

loose crown, wide spreading

The ripe reddish-brown fruits often remain on the tree until right into the winter. American settlers used to roast the seeds as a coffee substitute, when necessary, and brew a beer-like drink from the fruit. Nowadays the Honey Locust grows as an ornamental tree in city centres, since it is very undemanding and can tolerate polluted air.

Habitat Originates from North America. Found in gardens, parks and on roadsides of Europe. Trunk and branches have twig-like thorns.

> leaves pinnate or bi-pinnate
> yellow early autumn colouring
> thornless variety also exists

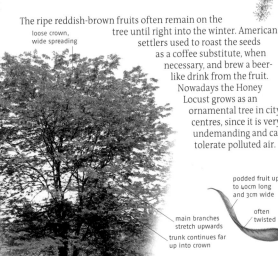

podded fruit up to 40cm long and 3cm wide

often twisted

main branches stretch upwards

trunk continues far up into crown

pinnate leaf with 20–34 leaflets

up to 2cm long, pointed, shiny green

Locust-tree
Ceratonia siliqua (legume family)
H 4–10m August–October

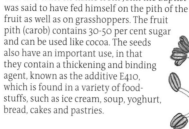

male flowers with 5 red stamens

Habitat *Found in the Mediterranean region in evergreen, broad-leaved forests and shrubberies, on rocks or in plantations. Flowers emerge straight from the branch itself.*

> originates from southern Asia
> old trees have bizarre appearance
> male and female trees

This tree takes its name from John the Baptist who was said to have fed himself on the pith of the fruit as well as on grasshoppers. The fruit pith (carob) contains 30-50 per cent sugar and can be used like cocoa. The seeds also have an important use, in that they contain a thickening and binding agent, known as the additive E410, which is found in a variety of food-stuffs, such as ice cream, soup, yoghurt, bread, cakes and pastries.

leathery leaves, evergreen, dark shiny green

leaflets arranged in 4–10 pairs

numerous lentil-like seeds

brown pith

fruit 10–30cm long

flat and compressed

144

spreading crown, dense foliage

trunk often very thick

Did you know?
When the seeds are ripe they weigh almost always 0.2g. Because of this consistency they were once used as a set measure for gold and gemstones, known as 'Carat'. Even today the 0.2g carat is the unit of weight for gemstones – as far as gold is concerned, however, carat is now a measure of purity.

Pagoda Tree

Sophora japonica (pea family)
H 12–20m August–September

Substances can be extracted from the flowers of the Pagoda Tree that act as an effective drug against poor circulation. In traditional Chinese medicine, the bark and seeds are used as well as the flowers for special compounds. The fruit is extremely toxic and is said to be acidic.

spherical crown, sometimes umbrella-like or even with several parts

usually appears loose

Habitat *Originates from northern China and Korea. Found in parks, squares and on roadsides in Europe. Fruit hangs from tree like strings of beads.*

> *very distinctive due to late flowering season and prolific flowers*
> *resembles the False Acacia (p. 147) but without thorns*
> *poisonous!*

suspended fruit pods

tightly clasped between seeds

leaf odd-pinnate with up to 17 leaflets

smooth margin

oval leaflet

yellowish-white flowers, up to 2cm in size

145

Yellow-wood

Cladrastis lutea (pea family)
H 8–15m May–June

American settlers used to boil up the wood from this tree to extract its yellow colouring and use it to dye fabrics. The twigs are very brittle, which is the reference to its scientific name, *Cladrastis*. This is derived from the Greek 'klados' meaning twig and 'rhaio' meaning to break. Consequently the tree is best suited only to those locations which are sheltered from the wind.

crown roundish

Habitat *Originates from the eastern side of North America. Grows in parks in Europe. Fruit pods hang between large distinctive leaves.*

> *leaves like Common Ash (p.154), but are alternate*
> *flowers with pleasant fragrance*
> *does not flower every year*

white pea-flowers

one or multiple stems

leaf odd-pinnate, up to 40cm long

leaflets not directly opposite

Common Laburnum

Laburnum anagyroides (pea family)
H 5–7m May–June

Habitat Native to southern Europe. In parks and gardens of central Europe, occasionally in the wild. Numerous yellow flowers hanging in clusters.

> - grows as tree or shrub
> - requires sufficient warmth and light
> - other names include 'Bean Tree' or 'Golden Rain Tree'

The wood of the Common Laburnum tends to creak on hot summer days. This noise is caused by the fruits which split open as they dry out. The entire tree is extremely poisonous. Since the peeled-off bark and fruits smell somewhat like peas, children in particular are tempted to eat them. Poisoning causes bloody vomiting, dizziness, cramp and can be fatal due to respiration paralysis.

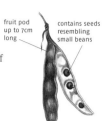

fruit pod up to 7cm long

contains seeds resembling small beans

Did you know?

The very hard timber, which is yellow to dark brown in colour, yields a beautiful grain. It was once used to make musical instruments, crossbow arrows and lathed wooden objects.

oval leaflet up to 8cm long

trifoliate leaves

bright yellow flowers

with one or mostly multiple stems

high growth, irregular

branches initially upright, later on overhanging

False Acacia
Robinia pseudoacacia (pea family)
H 10–25m May–June

This tree's roots have small nodules on them containing bacteria which absorb nitrogen from the air. This supply of nutrients means that the tree can be found growing on very poor soils. Its name often leads to confusion with the true acacias (p. 142). The flowers contain a lot of nectar to which bees are attracted. For every kilo of 'acacia honey' the bees must draw nectar from around 1,600,000 flowers.

Habitat *Originates from North America. Frequently planted on roadsides, in parks and on slopes. Flowers form white distinctive clusters*

> **extremely poisonous!**
> **flowers have a pleasant, sweet fragrance**
> **leaflets point downwards at night**

loose, irregular crown

flat fruits up to 10cm long

4–10 dark brown seeds

pea-flowers, up to 2cm long

odd-pinnate leaf with up to 23 leaflets

underside lighter in colour

base often has 2 thorns

147

woody thorns remain on twigs

often squarrose branches

Did you know?
*Occasionally the Clammy Locust (*Robinia viscosa*) is found growing in parks and gardens. It has pink flowers and its shoots, flower stalks and fruits are sticky. This tree also originates from North America.*

deeply furrowed bark

one or multiple stems

Amur Cork Tree

Phellodendron amurense (rue family)
H 10–15m June

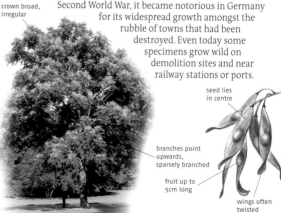

loose crown

Habitat Found growing in eastern Asia, particularly in the Amur region. Occasionally in parks in Europe. Panicles with fruit up to 1cm long.

> opposite leaves
> requires slightly damp soil
> fruits smell of turpentine when crushed

Alongside the Cork Oak (p. 93), the Amur Cork Tree is the most important source of cork, which is used particularly for insulation materials. Specific preparatory methods in Chinese medicine mean that it can produce some of the most significant traditional remedies. These are deployed by experienced therapists for a whole range of illnesses.

main branches stretch upwards

odd-pinnate leaf with 9–13 leaflets
bluish underneath

thick, grey, corky, deeply furrowed bark

short trunk

long, extended leaf tips

148

flowers up to 1cm across in upright panicles

Tree of Heaven

Ailanthus altissima (tree-of-heaven family)
H 20–25m June–July

Habitat Native to China. Often growing wild in central Europe in parks and gardens. Usually develops plenty of fruit.

> leaves have strong, unpleasant smell, somewhat rubbery
> usually with several trunks or with young shoots growing from the roots
> only lives for 50–60 years

This tree can tolerate aridness, smoke and exhaust fumes. It is therefore ideal for re-forestation on steppe areas. After the Second World War, it became notorious in Germany for its widespread growth amongst the rubble of towns that had been destroyed. Even today some specimens grow wild on demolition sites and near railway stations or ports.

crown broad, irregular

seed lies in centre

odd-pinnate leaf with 13–31 leaflets, up to 60cm long

pinnate leaf with 1–2 teeth, also on underside

branches point upwards, sparsely branched

fruit up to 5cm long

wings often twisted

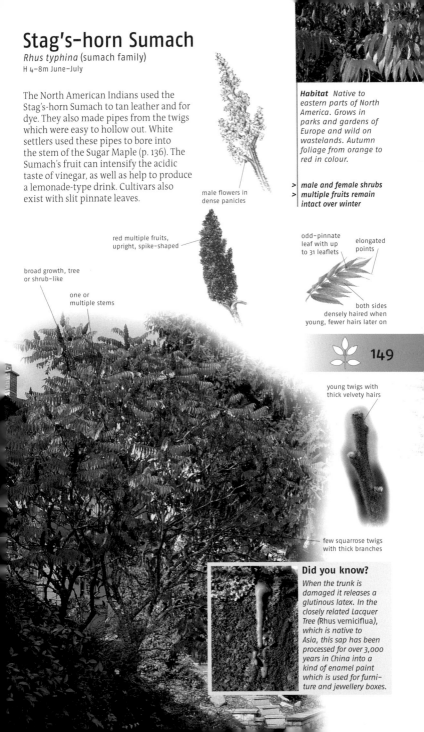

Stag's-horn Sumach

Rhus typhina (sumach family)

H 4–8m June–July

The North American Indians used the Stag's-horn Sumach to tan leather and for dye. They also made pipes from the twigs which were easy to hollow out. White settlers used these pipes to bore into the stem of the Sugar Maple (p. 136). The Sumach's fruit can intensify the acidic taste of vinegar, as well as help to produce a lemonade-type drink. Cultivars also exist with slit pinnate leaves.

Habitat *Native to eastern parts of North America. Grows in parks and gardens of Europe and wild on wastelands. Autumn foliage from orange to red in colour.*

> *male and female shrubs*
> *multiple fruits remain intact over winter*

male flowers in dense panicles

red multiple fruits, upright, spike-shaped

odd-pinnate leaf with up to 31 leaflets

elongated points

both sides densely haired when young, fewer hairs later on

broad growth, tree or shrub-like

one or multiple stems

149

young twigs with thick velvety hairs

few squarrose twigs with thick branches

Did you know?

When the trunk is damaged it releases a glutinous latex. In the closely related Lacquer Tree (Rhus verniciflua), which is native to Asia, this sap has been processed for over 3,000 years in China into a kind of enamel paint which is used for furniture and jewellery boxes.

California Peppertree

Schinus molle (sumach family)
H 5–10m April–August

broad, irregular crown

Habitat *Originates from dry areas of central and southern America. Grown in the Mediterranean as an ornamental tree. Dried fruits produce 'red peppercorns'.*

> **evergreen**
> **leaves and fruits smell aromatic when crushed**
> **tolerates heat and aridness**

The red fruit of the California Peppertree is often used alongside the black, white and green grains of the Black Pepper (*Piper nigrum*) in mixes of colourful peppercorns, such as those used in glass pepper mills. It is not however closely related to the Black Pepper. Its fruits have a sharp taste despite their aromatic quality which not everyone likes.

pinnate leaf, 10–30cm long

19–41 narrow leaflets

hanging branches

tiny pink to red fruits on hanging stalks

flowers up to 1cm in size in large panicles

4, occasionally 5 brilliant yellow crown-like leaves

Pride-of-India

Koelreuteria paniculata (pride-of-India family)
H 5–8m July–August

loose crown, fairly small, roundish to umbrella-shaped

Habitat *Native to Japan, Korea and China. Grows in parks and gardens in central Europe. The distinctive multiple fruits jut out from the foliage.*

> **fruit capsules develop very rapidly**
> **distinctive during both flowering and fruit-bearing season**
> **yellow autumn foliage**

The name *Koelreuteria* pays tribute to the botanist from Karlsruhe, Joseph Gottlieb Koelreuter, who lived in the 18th century. He recognised the important role that insects play in plant pollination and finally proved the fact that plants also reproduce sexually.

usually with multiple stems, trunk often short

odd-pinnate leaf

often pinnate again at base

lobed leaflets or pinnatifid

papery wall

inflated, lantern-like fruits up to 5cm long, with 3 black spherical seeds

Bead Tree

Melia azedarach (mahogany family)

H 5–15m April–June

The flowers of this tree, also known as the 'Persian Lilac', smell strongly of lilac, especially in the evening. They attract moths. The fruit kernels, which have an interesting angular shape, were once threaded into rosaries. Presumably, this is why the tree was also known as the 'Holy Tree'. Its timber is suitable for furniture and carving.

Habitat *Native to the Himalayas. Grown as an ornamental tree on estates and roadsides in the Mediterranean. Fruit remains on tree for a long time.*

> *leaves can also be pinnate*
> *poisonous fruit!*
> *quite hardy*

5 or 6 petals

petal about 2cm across

stamens form a tube

yellow fruit, about 1cm thick

stone fruit woody, edged

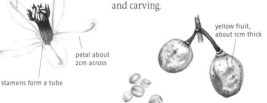

bi-pinnate leaf, 30–60cm long

oval to elliptical-shaped leaflets

margin sharply serrated

151

main branches stretch upwards, sparsely twigged

very loose crown

usually with multiple stems

Did you know?

The closely related Neem Tree (Antelaea azadirachta) has smooth, elongated stone fruits. Processing methods of both stones and fruit have resulted in the production of an effective alternative to chemical pesticides and this product has been on the market for some years now.

Paper-bark Maple

Acer griseum (maple family)
H 5–12m April–May

2 samaras

wings lie at acute or right angles to each other

crown round to oval, usually regular

Habitat *Native to China. Grows in parks and collections. Characteristic cinnamon-coloured bark peels off in paper-thin flakes.*

> *reddish-orange autumn foliage*
> *should be grown as a single tree*

The Paper-bark Maple is named after its characteristic bark. Even on very thin branches it unravels, and on thick stems it peels off in many different layers at the same time. This gives the impression that the stem is wrapped with thin paper. As the tree is undemanding and is very attractive even when still young, it is ideal for domestic gardens.

leaflet up to 6cm long

margin roughly serrated

trifoliate leaf

single or often with several trunks from far below

152

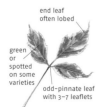

Box Maple

Acer negundo (maple family)
H 10–20m March–April

female flowers in hanging clusters

2 samaras

wings mainly V-shaped

Habitat *Originates from eastern part of North America. Grows in grounds and parks, also wild. Fruits form hanging clusters.*

> *male and female trees*
> *tolerates aridness*
> *numerous garden varieties*

At first glance, the leaves in particular, as well as the male flowers and multiple fruits of this tree resemble the Common Ash (p. 154). The flowers emerge before the leaves which makes the male ones particularly distinctive because of their prolific abundance. The pollen is blown onto the female flowers by the wind.

end leaf often lobed

green or spotted on some varieties

odd-pinnate leaf with 3–7 leaflets

male flowers with long stalks, in clusters

wide crown, also irregular and squarrose with age

one or multiple stems

Manna Ash

Fraxinus ornus (ash family)

H 5–15m May–June

In early history the Greeks used to make lances and spears from the wood of this tree. Nemesis, the Greek goddess of justice, carried a branch of the tree in her hand as a symbol for her fair decisions. Despite the fact that the tree yields 'manna' (see box), the 'manna' described in the Bible is said to have come not from the Manna Ash, but from one of the desert lichens.

fruits up to 4cm long, hang in bundles

long wing

Habitat Grows wild in southern Europe, especially in mountainous and limestone regions. Found in parks of central Europe. Fragrant flowers form loose, feathery clusters.

> flowering trees look white from a distance
> fruits often remain on tree over winter

circular crown, densely branched

odd-pinnate leaf, up to 25cm long

lighter colour underneath

serrated margin

7–9 short stemmed leaflets

153

Did you know?

When the trunk or branches are damaged, a sap is released which hardens on contact with the air. This yellowish-white 'manna' is sweet to taste even though it contains little sugar. As well as being a sweetening agent, it is also used as a remedy for coughs and constipation.

one or multiple stems

Common Ash

Fraxinus excelsior (ash family)
H 15–35m April–May

brownish flowers
in panicles

Habitat *Wild in woods near riverside meadows and gorges, alongside streams, rivers, rocks. Distinctive black buds in winter.*

> *leaves opposite*
> *flowers appear before leaves*
> *grows in very damp and dry locations*

The strong winter wind brings the fruit spinning off the tree. Because of its sheer size, the Vikings used to compare the world to a giant ash –'Yggdrasil' or World Ash. The bark of the Ash is one of the oldest substitutes for cinchona bark and was once used for the treatment of malaria.

crown slender, oval to almost roundish

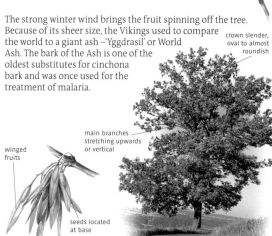

main branches stretching upwards or vertical

odd-pinnate leaf with 9–15 leaflets

serrated margin

winged fruits

seeds located at base

Red Buckeye

Aesculus pavia (horse-chestnut family)
H 6–10m May–June

4 dissimilar red petals

calyx with hairy glands

Habitat *Native to North America. Occasionally in parks in Europe. Panicles with fewer flowers overtopping branches.*

> *often only shrub-like growth*
> *also grafted as a tall tree*
> *buds not sticky*

horizontal or hanging branches

The Red Buckeye is one of the parents to the Red Horse Chestnut (p. 156). Its name pays tribute to the Dutch botanist Peter Paaw, who lived towards the end of the 16th century and also went under the name of Peter Pavius. The tree is susceptible to the Horse Chestnut leaf miner (see following species), but is not as affected as the Horse Chestnut.

irregularly serrated margin

5–7 stemmed leaflets, 8–14cm long

leaves palmately compound

spineless

brown seed

oval capsulate fruit

with one or multiple stems

Horse Chestnut

Aesculus hippocastanum (horse-chestnut family)

H 15–35m April–May

Gardeners have been planting this tree in Europe since 1646. To begin with it only grew in stately parks and avenues. Nowadays with its shade-giving crown, it has become a tree typically found in beer gardens. In times of need, the seeds were rendered less bitter and used to make cooking oil and flour. Even the Turks used to feed the fruits to their horses (hence the name!). Nowadays they are used for game fodder. Some drugs for weak veins and 'heavy leg' syndrome also contain extracts from them.

flowers up to 2cm in size

white with yellow or red markings

upright spherical flower stem

heavily spined

spherical fruit capsule, up to 6cm in size

shiny, dark brown seeds

crown rounded off at top

broad crown

Habitat *Naturally occurring in the Balkans. Cultivated on roadsides, squares and in parks of central and western Europe. Seeds dispersed in September and October.*

> **emerging leaves have thick woolly hairs**
> **buds very sticky, especially at the end of winter**
> **popular tree for beer gardens**

leaf palmately compound

leaflets broadest in top third

5–7 unstemmed leaflets up to 20cm long

155

protruding branches, branches of older trees overhang

Did you know?

Small larvae can be seen using backlit photography on the brown spots that often appear on the leaves. As a result, the leaves fall off. The larvae are those of the Horse Chestnut leaf miner, a moth that first appeared in Europe in 1984 and has since become extremely widespread.

Red Horse Chestnut
Aesculus x *carnea* (horse-chestnut family)
H 10–15m May

Habitat *Only known as a cultivated variety. In European parks, on roadsides and estate grounds. Red flowers in distinctive panicles.*

> *later flowering than the Horse Chestnut*
> *only develops a few fruits*
> *often grafted as a tall-stemmed tree*

This tree is a hybrid of the Horse Chestnut itself and the Red Buckeye that emerged about the beginning of the 19th century. Some varieties are scarcely affected by the Horse Chestnut leaf miner and so are good alternatives. Although the moth lays its eggs on the leaves, the young larvae mainly die off.

broad crown, dome-shaped

densely compact

no or very few spines

light red flowers, up to 2cm in size

leaf palmately compound

lighter-coloured underneath

shiny dark green on top

5–7 almost 'sessile' leaflets

Jacaranda Tree
Jacaranda mimosifolia (bignonia family)
H 10–16m July

bluish-purple bell-shaped flowers

Habitat *Native to South American Tropics. In southern Europe as an ornamental and roadside tree. Flower clusters, up to 30cm long.*

> *fruits remain on tree for a long time*
> *flowers appear before foliage*
> *requires warmth*

The Jacaranda Tree in its flowering season is one of the most beautiful and distinctive roadside trees of southern Europe. Its fruits are also decorative and are popular in flower arrangements. Closely related trees such as the *Jacaranda brasiliana* and the *Jacaranda obtusifolia* yield palisander wood, a very expensive tropical forest timber which is used for pianos and valuable furniture.

broad growth

opens with 2 flaps

samaras

woody fruit capsules

with one or multiple stems

bipinnate leaf, 30–40cm long

Elder

Sambruscus nigra (honeysuckle family)
H 2–7m June

Tea made from the flowers of this tree has a sudorific effect for feverish colds and alleviates irritable coughing. The juice of the fruit is rich in vitamins and minerals. However, fresh fruits may also cause vomiting and diarrhoea, particularly amongst children. The Germanic peoples actually consecrated the Elder as a sacred tree of the lady Holle (Freya), goddess of the home. The Irish, on the other hand, thought that witches rode through the air on broomsticks made of Elder branches.

Habitat Wild nearly all over Europe in damp soil on edges of woods, in hedges and on disturbed ground. Inflorescences up to 15cm across and strong-smelling.

> **opposite leaves, with unpleasant odour when crushed**
> **indicates nitrogen in soil**
> **flowering only in light locations**

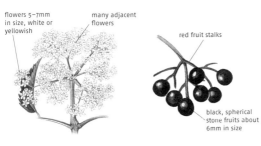

flowers 5–7mm in size, white or yellowish

many adjacent flowers

red fruit stalks

black, spherical stone fruits about 6mm in size

pinnate leaf with mainly 5, less commonly, 7 or 9 leaflets

serrated margin

157

very dense growth

shrub-like or tree-like

usually with multiple stems

Did you know?

The Judas' Ear Fungus (Hirneola auricula-judae) grows frequently on weakened Elder trunks. This is a mushroom which is hard when dry and tough and gelatinous when wet. It is known as 'Mu Err' or 'Ear Mushrooms' in Chinese restaurants.

Dwarf Fan Palm

Chamaerops humulis (palm family)
H 1–10m March–April

1–3cm long fruits, fairly firm

Habitat *Wild in Sicily and southern Spain. Cultivated in parks in southern regions and as a pot plant in central Europe. Characteristic thorny leaf stalk.*

> inedible fruits
> grows only as a shrub on heavily grazed land
> inhabits dry, exposed locations

This palm is particularly special in that it is not only cultivated in, but also native to Europe. The leaves yield fibres which are ideal for using as mattress filling and for upholstered furniture. Palms were growing in Europe up to two million years ago but it became too cold for them during the Ice Ages.

leaves form a tuft at end of stem

fan-shaped leaf blade, up to 80cm wide

long stalk, densely thorned

stem covered in fibres, concealed on small palms by leaves

158

Chusan Palm

Trachycarpus fortunei (palm family)
H 4–10m June–July

flower clusters surrounded by sheath

Habitat *Originates from northern China and Japan. Often cultivated in the Mediterranean and warm locations. Bright inflorescences.*

> leaf blades tear into strips in the wind
> most frequently cultivated palm in Europe
> inedible fruits

leaves form a tuft at end of stem

The extremely robust Chusan Palm not only grows in nearly every park in southern regions of Europe, it can even last the entire winter in the open air in warm locations that lie further north. The trunks are densely covered with a fibrous net of rotted leaf stalks that protects the actual trunk. Mats and ropes were once produced from the tough fibres.

fruits blue when ripe, up to 2cm thick

fan-shaped leaf blade

stem only lightly toothed

stem covered in fibres, concealed on small palms by leaves

Canary Palm

Phoenix canariensis (palm family)

H 8–20m February–June

leaves form a thick tuft
at end of trunk

The Canary Palm is a faster grower than the Date Palm and is a lot more tolerant of the cold. Consequently it could survive as an ornamental tree. The palm leaves produce characteristic decorations for Palm Sunday in the Christian calendar and for the Feast of Tabernacles in the Jewish.

Habitat Native to the Canary Islands. Ornamental tree in the whole of the Mediterranean. Light-coloured inflorescences contain masses of flowers.

> as a rule, a denser crown than the Date Palm
> very deep-rooted
> fruit contains virtually no flesh, therefore without nutritional value

sharp-angled leaves

single trunk

golden brown fruit around 2cm in size

central leaflets up to 50cm long

pinnate palm leaf, 5–6m long

Date Palm

Phoenix dactylifera (palm family)

H 10–30m February–June

leaves form a thick tuft at end of trunk

The Date Palm yields so-called 'desert bread' in the oases of Africa. It produces nutritious fruits that either taste sweet or mealy depending on their quality. Camels can even make good use of the hard fibrous kernels. The wood from the trunk is used for building and the leaves for covering houses.

Habitat Originally from the Arabian regions. Only seldom cultivated in the European Mediterranean. Characteristic tree of the Sahara oases.

> male and female trees
> can tolerate measures of salt
> requires heat and intolerant of humid air

high growth, also with multiple stems

fruit, 'dates' up to 8cm long

hard kernel

central leaflets up to 40cm long

pinnate palm leaf, 3–5m long

Savine

Juniperus sabina (juniper family)
H 0.5–2m April–May

young needle-like
leaves, 4–5mm long

Habitat Wild in mountainous regions, from Europe as far as central Asia. Ornamental shrub in gardens, parkland areas and cemeteries. Fruit distinctively blue and pruinose.

> tolerates sun and dryness
> twigs have revolting odour when crushed
> upright-growing variety also exists for gardens

In the Middle Ages the Savine was used as a healing plant for asthma, lung illnesses and worms. It was also known as a method of performing abortions, but more often than not resulted in the death of mother and child. Poisoning leads to convulsions and kidney and liver damage. Should the plant sap come into contact with the skin, it can cause inflammation.

scaly leaves
1–3 mm long

with elongated gland

irregular spherical berry cone, 3–7mm in size

blue pruinose

broad, dense growth

branches usually low-lying

Phoenician Juniper

Juniperus phoenicea (juniper family)
H 0.5–8m February–June

growth mainly very bushy

Habitat Wild in the Mediterranean in forests and on scrubland, particularly near coastal areas. Fruit ripens in the second year.

> can live up to 1,000 years
> can display quite diverse growth patterns
> very undemanding

It is extremely rare to find trees of up to 8m that have short, very strong trunks. These were once valued for building and joinery, but many were also felled for firewood and destroyed by intensive grazing and fire. In Spain the Phoenician Juniper is one of the most important fodder plants of wild mountain goats.

very dense

scaly leaves
1–2mm long

packed closely together on twig in roofing tile formation

berry cone 0.8–1.5cm thick

yellow to reddish-brown when ripe

Sea Grape

Ephedra distachya (sea grape family)
H 0.4–1m May–June

The substance ephedrine, which comes from the Sea Grape, is effective for asthma sufferers. However the plant is not wholly safe. The plant has also spread into the world of drugs under the name of 'Herbal Ecstasy' or 'Cloud 9'. In the United States of America, quite a number of people have already died from its abuse. It is also offered to help build up muscles or to curb the appetite.

masses of thin, mainly curved twigs

rod-like twigs

Habitat Wild in southern Europe and on the French Atlantic coast in sand and riverbanks. Thin greyish-green twigs are characteristic.

> **twigs easily broken**
> **resembles the Horse-tail**
> **male and female plants**

spherical adjacent male flowers

twigs often parallel pointing in one direction

red fleshy cones 6–7mm in size

inconspicuous greyish-white scaly leaves

green, grooved twigs

Gorse

Ulex europaeus (pea family)
H 0.6–2m April–June

It is particularly on pasture land in the British Isles that the Gorse has become a troublesome 'weed'. Due to stringent controls to curb the infestation of rabbits, the Gorse's natural enemy has been decimated. Grazing animals avoid this thorny plant and the wood is extremely poisonous to humans.

Habitat Wild in western Europe from Portugal to Great Britain. Rarely cultivated in central Europe. Single flowers on and between thorns.

> **thorns act as protection**
> **requires mild winters**
> **dies right back in severe winters in central Europe**

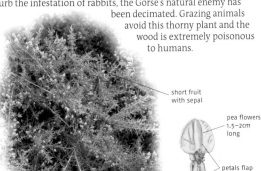

short fruit with sepal

pea flowers 1.5–2cm long

petals flap open wide apart

squarrose form

leaves and short shoots formed into thorns

rigid twiggy thorns

Rosemary

Rosmarinus officinalis (dead-nettle family)
H 0.3–1.5m March–July

Habitat Wild in the Mediterranean and in garden tubs in central Europe. Its lovely flowers make it an ornamental plant as well as a practical one.

> entire plant smells strong
> as a herb, aids digestion
> different cultivated varieties exist

Rosemary is the ideal seasoning for meat and potato dishes. In bath products, it helps the circulation. In one tradition it stood as a symbol for love and was used to decorate tables at weddings and in flower garlands for the bridal pair. In another it was part of the cult of the dead: the people who are left behind would strew Rosemary twigs into the grave as a symbol of remembrance and in the hope of new birth. Even today in some regions, coffin-bearers wear sprigs of Rosemary.

Did you know?
It was once thought that Rosemary improved the memory and preserved youth. This probably derived from the fact that the dried leaves retain their fragrance throughout the year. In order to remember an important personal day, people used to pick Rosemary leaves on that day and keep them.

slender, linear leaf, up to 4cm long

curled-up margin

underside white and downy

mainly pale blue flowers, about 1cm long

2 protruding stamens

lower lip with dark, mottled pattern

bushy growth with upright branches

densely leaved

flowers along twigs

Bog-rosemary

Andromeda polifolia (heather family)
H 0.1–0.3m May–August

flower corolla spherical to
oval, 0.5–0.8cm long

Andromeda is, in Greek mythology, the
daughter of Cassiopeia. According to legend,
both were placed as stars in heaven, in the
same part of the sky that
embraces the distribution
area of the Bog-
rosemary. The plant
contains toxins
which lower the
blood pressure
and can lead
to respiratory
paralysis.

Habitat *Wild in the
high moorlands of
north and central
Europe. Found on
nutrient-deficient
soil, often in layers
of sphagnum moss.
Flowers situated at end
of sprigs.*

> *evergreen leaves*
> *looks like buried bran-
> ches of Rosemary (p. 162)*
> *main axils creeping over
> ground*

upright
branches

alternate leaves

coarse leaf,
1–4cm long

underside
bluish-
green,
hairless

curled-up
margin

Alpine Heather

Erica carnea (heather family)
H 0.1–0.4m January–April

sepal shorter
than corolla

crown cylindrical
to jug-shaped,
5–7mm long

protruding anthers

The flower buds of the Alpine Heather are already
formed in autumn. The plant is popularly cultivated
in many varieties in gardens as a winter-flowerer
and evergreen ground coverage. There are yellow-
leafed varieties and the flowers range from white to deep purple.
Whereas most members of the heather family require acid soil,
Alpine Heather manages in alkaline conditions.

Habitat *Wild in the
mountainous regions
of central and southern
Europe. Commonly
planted in gardens.
Distinctive due to its
unusual flowering
season.*

> *also known as 'Winter
> Heather'*
> *prefers sunny locations*
> *some varieties flower in
> October*

flowers usually pointing to one side

low to
creeping growth

flowers nodding, in
dense clusters

needle-like leaves,
6–10mm long

in whorls of 3–4

Scotch Heather

Calluna vulgaris (heather family)

H 0.2–0.8m July–September

Habitat Wild all over Europe on moorland, poor acidic pastureland and in bogs and open Pine forests. Flowers normally point to one side.

> - leaves evergreen
> - suitable for dried flower arrangements
> - also known as 'Broom' or 'Besom Heather'

Scotch Heather can transform whole areas of land into a carpet of pink flowers. As a result, in its flowering season, it attracts hordes of people to places such as the Lüneburg Heathland in Germany. Where it grows, the soil quality deteriorates in time, in such a way that trees become established either late or not at all. Bees collect the nectar from the flowers to make 'Heather honey'. The twigs were once used for making brooms that were extremely durable.

pinkish sepal 4mm long

corolla petals half as long as sepal

scaly leaves, opposite, 2–4mm long

overlapping like roof tiles

densely twigged

branches partly low-lying, partly upright

clusters with many flowers

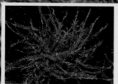

Did you know?

There are many different garden varieties of Scotch Heather. They differ both in their growth pattern and also in the colour of the leaves and flowers. When cultivating them, it is worth noting that they all require alkaline-free soil.

Prickly Pear

Opuntia ficus-indica (cactus family)

H 2–5m April–July

The Spanish brought the Prickly Pear over to the Mediterranean following the discovery of America. Separated from the succulent outer layer, the fruit has a sweet taste and is found over here as an edible fruit. The juicy segments are good as animal fodder. When cooked for a short while, even the thorny segments themselves can be used. In dry areas of agricultural land, it also acts as a hedge plant.

Habitat Native to the American Tropics. Planted in and naturalised in the Mediterranean. Segments unmistakeable, even from a distance.

> *requires sun and tolerates severe aridness*
> *germinative seeds*
> *small parts develop into new plants*

sunken-in at top

5–9cm large fig-like fruit

prickly cushion

made up of misshapen oval segments

pruinose, bluish-green

cushion-like groups with small bristles

flat, fleshy segments

under 1cm long thorns

165

juicy fruit flesh

small seeds

upright growth, squarrose

flower 6–10cm across

many yellow or orange petals

numerous stamens

Did you know?

This species is a host-plant for scale insects which produce a vivid red dye. This 'cochineal' is the food colouring agent found in Campari under the abbreviation E120. Some lipsticks also take their colour from cochineal.

Retuse-leaved Willow

Salix retusa (willow family)
H 0.05–0.25m June–July

Habitat Wild in the mountainous regions of central and south-eastern Europe. On stony ground up to altitudes of 2,500m. In the fruit-bearing season, the plant is covered with hairy seeds.

> **margin occasionally or loosely serrated**
> **often covers stones**
> **commonly found in snow-covered locations**

In autumn the leaves turn vivid yellow and give off an extremely strange smell, almost like Valerian. The creeping surface branches then form roots wherever there is a suitable surface present, such as in a crevice or cracks in a rocky plain. In places where the plant creeps over any loose rubble, it manages to secure it effectively.

Did you know?

All of the woody twigs grow under-ground on the related Dwarf Willow (*Salix herbacea*). The short overground shoots with the finely notched margin remain herbaceous. The naturalist Linnaeus described this plant as 'the smallest tree in the world'.

leaves form clusters

oval leaf, 1–3cm long

tip usually rounded-off

catkins surrounded by leaves

far-reaching creeping surface branches

numerous off-shoots

166

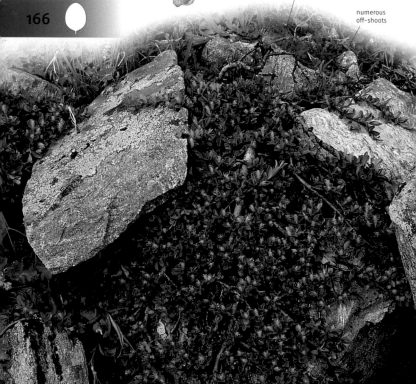

Net-leaved Willow

Salix reticulata (willow family)

H 0.1–0.3m July–August

The Net-leaved Willow, just like the Retuse-leaved Willow and the Dwarf Willow (opposite page), is one of the alpine willows. They grow so high up in the mountains or in the north, that they are covered by snow for long periods. Despite this, they still manage to flower and develop seeds in the short growing season.

Habitat Wild in northern Europe and in mountainous regions of central and southern Europe. Usually above the tree line up to 3,000m. Leaves appear wrinkled.

catkins elongated and cylindrical, up to 1.5cm

low-lying creeping branches

> *can form large mats*
> *branches develop roots in the soil*
> *grows on open, stony ground and rubble*

leaf 2–5cm long, round to widely oval

leaves with woolly hairs at first

distinctive deep veins

underside with dense hairs

167

Star Magnolia

Magnolia stellata (magnolia family)

H 1.5–3m March–April

Whereas the majority of magnolias mainly grow into large trees (p. 64, 65), the Star Magnolia remains small and is therefore ideal in sheltered locations in small gardens. It has been planted in Japan now for centuries but did not arrive in Europe until the second half of the 19th century.

delicate growth

flowers even as young tree

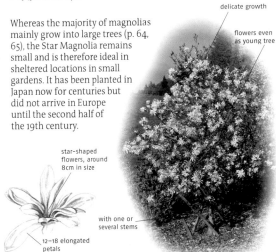

Habitat Originates from Japan. Found in Europe in more sheltered locations in gardens and parks. Flowers are white or pink.

> *grows relatively slowly*
> *flowers susceptible to night frost*
> *named after shape of its flowers*

star-shaped flowers, around 8cm in size

with one or several stems

12–18 elongated petals

leaf up to 10cm long, inverted oval

wavy margin

Californian Allspice

Calycanthus occidentalis (spicebush family)
H 1–4m June–July

tips soon turn yellowish-brown

brownish-red catkins, internal ones bigger than external

Habitat Native to California. Found in parks and gardens of Europe as a hardy tree. Characteristic brownish-red star-shaped flowers.

> flowers last for many days
> lovely as individual tree
> related Eastern Sweet-shrub has dark reddish-brown flowers

The flowers smell strongly of fruit wine and spicy gingerbread and the dried bark of cloves. The Cherokee Indians once used parts of the bark of the closely related Eastern Sweetshrub (*Calycanthus floridus*) as a spice as well as for emetics and medicine. Care must be taken, however, in doing this, as the wood contains toxins, which are particularly strong in the seeds.

topside particularly rough

pointed tip

leaf narrow and oval, up to 20cm long

widespread and dense growth

Wintersweet

Chimonanthus praecox (spicebush family)
H 2–4m February–March

Habitat Originates from China. In parks and gardens of European regions with mild winters. Numerous nodding flowers are very distinctive.

> opposite leaves
> fragrant flowers do not tolerate severe cold
> slightly susceptible to frost when young

Bees and flies are attracted to the intense fragrance of the Wintersweet's flowers in warm, early spring days and help its pollination. They find sweet nectar in the waxy flowers. When flowers or cut branches are brought indoors, their fragrance resembles Jasmine.

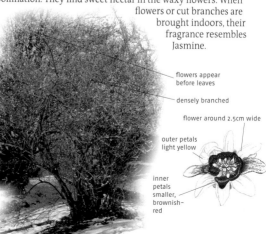

flowers appear before leaves

densely branched

flower around 2.5cm wide

outer petals light yellow

inner petals smaller, brownish-red

topside with short bristles

oval to lanceolate coarse leaf, 6–20cm long

Mistletoe

Viscum album (mistletoe family)
H 0.2–0.8m April–May

Mistletoe is a partial parasite. It bores a sucking device into the branch of the host tree with which it extracts water and nutritious salts. However, it can produce carbohydrates on its own as it possesses chlorophyll. The Celtic people held it in high regard as they believed it could ward off demons. In England, it is a longstanding tradition to hang Mistletoe at Christmas as a sign of enduring life.

berry-like fruit, pea-sized, entirely white

Habitat *Wild nearly all over Europe, found on deciduous trees, silver firs and pine trees. Often produces abundant fruit.*

yellowish inconspicuous flowers

> **male and female plants**
> **poisonous!**
> **seeds are dispersed by birds, such as the Mistle Thrush**

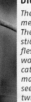

Did you know?

The Latin name Viscum *means 'birdlime'. The fruit contains a sticky, long thread-like flesh from which lime was once produced to catch birds. This gooey mass enables the seeds to stick onto the twigs where they can then germinate.*

fleshy leaf, 3–5cm long

shoots on every leaf pair

green or yellowish-green twigs, many of them forked

169

grows on branches of different trees

Japanese Barberry
Berberis thunbergii (barberry family)
H 1.5–2m May

thorn up to 1.5cm long

shiny red

berries less than 1cm long

Habitat Native to Japan. In gardens, parks and urban grounds. Fruit often remains on the bush until spring.

> very variable leaf shape
> impenetrable due to its many thorns
> ideal as hedge shrub

The Japanese Barberry is by far the most commonly planted barberry. There are many different varieties with leaf colours ranging from light yellow to deep red. The berries contain toxins which can be damaging to the kidneys. The harmless dried barberry fruit that is found in spice shops comes from the Common Barberry (p. 200).

very dense growth

commonly planted especially as reddish-brown leaf variety

yellow, exterior often red

thin leaf, 1–2cm long

flower up to 1cm in size

6 petals

170

Japanese Mock Orange
Pittosporum tobira (pittosporum family)
H 0.5–3m March–May

Habitat Originates from China and Japan. Found as a hedge shrub in southern Europe and as a tub plant in central Europe. Groups of whitish flowers on stem tips.

> evergreen
> fragrant flowers, smelling a little like Orange blossom
> tolerates dryness well

The seeds of the Japanese Mock Orange are embedded in a sticky, mucilaginous substance. This means that they stick onto birds' beaks, roaming animals and even onto humans, consequently increasing their distance of distribution.

fruit opens with 3 flaps

red seeds set in sticky substance

margin curls downwards

variety with mottled-white leaves

leaf 3–10cm long, leathery, shiny surface

light-coloured underside

leaves in groups at top of stems

Caper
Capparis spinosa (caper family)
H 0.3–1.5m April–October

The healers of the Ancient World used the buds and fruit from the Caper not only as a spice, but also as a possible cure for sciatica and cramp. The bark from the roots was also used for its healing properties. Nowadays farmers cultivate this bush particularly in southern France and Spain, in order to supply the food markets with this popular spice. The bushes can be regularly harvested for 30 to 40 years.

long fruit stalk

fleshy fruit capsule

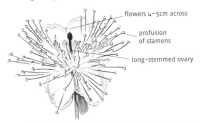

flowers 4–5cm across

profusion of stamens

long-stemmed ovary

Habitat *Wild on rocks, wasteland and on roadside verges in the central Mediterranean region. Ripe fruit bursts open, releasing masses of black seeds.*

> **stalks often low-lying or hanging**
> **partial climber**
> **flowers only open for a few hours**

tip with visible point

leaf broadly elliptical

Did you know?

Both the unopened flower buds as well as unripe fruits can be preserved in salt, vinegar or oil. They have a slightly peculiar, spicy and piquant aroma. The preserved fruits have a more intense flavour than the flower buds.

171

distinctive flowers in leaf axils, up to 7cm long

alternate leaves

Wall Cotoneaster
Cotoneaster horizontalis (rose family)
H 0.7–1.5m May–June

some hairs

red, pea-sized fruit

Blackbirds and other birds are attracted to the Wall Cotoneaster's fruit in autumn and winter as it is rich in nutrients. The birds digest the mealy fruit flesh and excrete the undigested seeds. These germinate so easily that this apecies is also found growing wild here in Europe.

Habitat *Native to central China. Commonly found in parks and gardens in Europe. Particularly distinctive in autumn due to its red leaves and abundant fruits.*

> easy to recognise due to its characteristic branches
> leaves fall later in year
> popular, hardy garden shrub

with fine point

leaf 0.5–1.2cm long, almost rounded

some hairs on underside and margin

flat, wide-spreading branches

branches in regular herring-bone formation

Willow-leaved Cotoneaster
Cotoneaster salicifolius (rose family)
H 2–3m June

many fruits packed close together

The leaves bear some resemblance to those of the Medlar (p. 112). Even though they are relatively small, the abundant flowers contain nectar with a high sugar content and pollen that is rich in protein. Consequently many insects, including honey bees, are attracted to them and aid pollination.

Habitat *Originates from China. Commonly planted in parks, gardens and estates in Europe. Fruit is usually abundant.*

> evergreen, though leaves with a reddish tinge
> fragrant flowers
> fruit remains on bush for a long time

red fruit, 4–6mm in diameter

broad growth with long, overhanging branches

copious multiple-flowered clusters with white flowers

leaf 4–8cm long, lanceolate

surface appears wrinkled

curled-up margin

underside downy

Box

Buxus sempervirens (box family)
H 0.3–4m April–May

In folklore the Box tree was said to possess protective and magical properties, as it was said to give protection from lightning and disease. The hard, heavy timber is used in the manufacture of pipe bowls, musical instruments and boxes. The word 'box' just like the French equivalent 'boîte' comes from the Latin word 'buxus'. Even the first slide rules, the 19th century forerunners of the modern calculator, were made out of boxwood.

Habitat *Wild in woods and undergrowth of southern Europe. Cultivated all over Europe in gardens and parks. Fruit with 6 points when opened up.*

Did you know?

Box trees can easily be pruned into ornamental features and figures and were therefore very popular during the Renaissance and Baroque periods. The custom to use Box also to edge garden beds dates back to the Romans, who originally brought this tradition to western and central Europe.

> **extremely slow-growing**
> **can reach an age of 600 years**
> **tolerates dryness and frost**

leathery, oval evergreen leaves, 1–2.5cm long

deflexed, curved margin

opposite

173

bushy growth

unopened fruit with 3 horns

yellowish-white flowers in clusters in leaf axils

shiny leaf surface

evergreen leaves, densely packed

Scotch Broom

Cytisus scoparius (pea family)
H 1–2m May–June

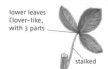

lower leaves
Clover-like,
with 3 parts

stalked

Habitat *Wild almost all over Europe on moorland, spinneys, on pathways and roadside verges. Flowers are either individual or in pairs.*

> **develops two sorts of early-falling leaves**
> **young branches with 5 edges**
> **deadly poisonous!**

upper leaves
single, up to
2cm long

The ripe fruit heats up in the sun and bursts open with a loud crack, and in doing so the seeds are flung out and scattered across several metres. Durable sweeping brooms were once made from the rough, tough branches. When used in precise measures, extracts of the Scotch Broom can help fight against heart and circulatory disorders.

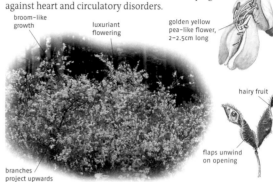

broom-like
growth

luxuriant
flowering

golden yellow
pea-like flower,
2–2.5cm long

hairy fruit

branches
project upwards

flaps unwind
on opening

174

Spanish Broom

Spartium junceum (pea family)
H 2–3m April–June

Habitat *Wild on scrubland and in open woodland in the Mediterranean. Also grown as an ornamental plant. Yellow flowers are positioned on rush-like stems.*

> **sparse leaves drop early**
> **round stems in plant cross-section**

bluish-green
lanceolate leaf,
1–3cm long

The pliable stems are good for making into hard-wearing baskets. They can also be used to obtain fibrous phloem and, years ago, ropemakers used this when making ropes for the shipping and fishing industries. The flowers were once used to counteract constipation, to help induce birth and as a treatment for gout. However, an overdose may prove fatal and even small measures may damage a person's genetic make-up.

opens
widely

pointed, grey to
bluish-green,
rod-like stems

fragrant pea-
flower, up to
2.5cm long

all stems
project
upwards

Dyer's Greenweed

Genista tinctoria (pea family)

H 0.3–0.7m June–August

Once an insect comes into contact with the flowers, they open wide apart and remain so. In the early English dyeing industry, Dyer's Greenweed was used as an important source of yellow dye. The thin twigs as well as both the flowers and leaves contain colouring substances. The colour they produce varies from lemon yellow to dark brown or olive green, depending on what has been added to it in the process.

Habitat Wild almost all over Europe on rough grassland, moorland, and woodland edges. Tops of stems are light green, not woody.

> upper stem sections die off in winter
> indicates nutrient-deficient locations
> poisonous!

Did you know?

The related Genista germanica or German Broom bears thorns on its older twigs. It grows in central and eastern Europe on moorland, heaths and on warm woodland edges.

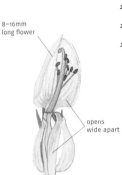

8–16mm long flower

opens wide apart

lanceolate leaf, 0.5–4.5cm long

175

only twigged near flowers

loose form

thornless twigs

Skimmia

Skimmia japonica (rue family)
H 0.5–2m April–May

4 or 5 petals

male flowers
with anthers

white, also
tinged with
red on
outside

Habitat *Native to Japan and China. In Europe in gardens, cemeteries, containers and pots. Usually develops many red, pea-sized fruits.*

> *male and female plants*
> *sweet fragrant flowers*
> *plant sap can cause skin irritation*

The Skimmia is extremely slow-growing and prefers moist soil in partial shade. In order to obtain as much fruit as possible, both male and female bushes should be grown. The fruit ripens from October onwards and can remain on the bush for up to a year – this makes it a truly decorative specimen, even in smaller gardens.

flowers and fruit often appear simultaneously

leaf up to 12cm long

in backlit photography with transparent specks

reddish stalk

evergreen leaves, in clusters on twig tips

Smoke Tree

Cotinus coggygria (sumach family)
H 2–5m June–July

Habitat *Wild in southern Europe in warm woodland areas and copses. In parks and gardens of central Europe. Leaves turn brilliant red in autumn.*

> *flowers release pleasant fragrance when crushed*
> *requires sunny locations*
> *leaves either greyish-green or dark red according to variety*

Most of the flowers are infertile and they drop from the tree. However, their stalks continue to grow and they develop projecting hairs. From this, protruding wig-like multiple fruits are formed, which can be dispersed by the wind. The yellow wood contains a colouring agent that is good for dyeing silk and leather.

growth appears dense

distinctive wig-like multiple fruits

5 white petals

flower stalk with numerous inconspicuous flowers

feathery, hairy stalks

leaf 3–4cm long, inverted oval, slender

long, thin stalk

flat fruit 3–5mm in size

Sea Buckthorn

Hippophae rhamnoides (sea–buckthorn family)
H 1–5m April–May

The name *Hippophae* is derived from the Greek words 'hippos' (horse) and 'phaos' (light). In the Ancient World, this referred to the fact that the shrub was used as an eye remedy for horses. In the 18th century, Linnaeus transferred this name over to the Sea Buckthorn. The fruits of the Sea Buckthorn contain a fatty oil and many vitamins and minerals. As juice, they strengthen the body's defences and help counter exhaustion. The oil from them is found in natural cosmetic products.

Habitat *Wild in mountainous areas of central and southern Europe, and by the North and Baltic Sea. Cultivated on roadsides and by reservoirs. Female shrub produces abundant fruit.*

> male and female shrubs
> fruit ripens from September to December
> tolerates soil containing salt

Did you know?

The fruit is especially eaten by pheasants but also by other birds. They excrete the hard, undigested seeds and in doing so ensure their dispersal. However the fruit often remains on the shrub, unnoticed, throughout the winter.

narrow leaf 2–8cm long

grey dots on surface

underside silvery white to copper red

2 sepals

male flowers with 4 anthers

orange fruit up to 8mm thick, with silvery scales

177

robust rigid thorn

upright growth, densely twigged, squarrose

branches appear rigid

Rock Rose

Cistus albidus (rock-rose family)
H 0.4m April–June

numerous
stamens

pink petals, up to 3cm
in size, with character-
istic crinkles

Habitat *Wild in the
western Mediterranean.
On scrubland and
in airy woods. Pink
flowers only open wide
in sunshine.*

> *opposite leaves*
> *from a distance
>   resembles a rose*
> *only flowers from
>   morning to early
>   afternoon*

The Rock Rose is generally white in colour
as its leaves have a white felt-like surface.
This acts as protection from the sun and stops
severe evaporation. It is therefore
well-suited to dry, sunny locations.
Other members of this family
like the Labdanum (see
below) develop
leathery leaves
containing resin
for the same
reason.

leaf 2–5cm long,
with white felt-
like hairs

dense growth,
often nearly
spherical

foliage has
whitish-green
appearance

3 parallel
veins

178

Labdanum

Cistus ladanifer (rock-rose family)
H 0.5–2.5m April–June

flower up to
10cm in size

5 petals with
crinkled look

dark red
spot at base

Habitat *Native to
southern France and
Spain. Commonly plant-
ed in southern Europe.
The distinctive flower
petals have a crinkled
appearance.*

> *opposite leaves*
> *plant feels sticky and
>   smells pleasantly
>   aromatic*
> *tolerates dryness well*

When any grazing goats pass
between these shrubs, the tacky
resin sticks onto their legs and
beards. In the olden days, this
used to be collected directly
from the goats themselves and
used for smoking and for
ointments. The perfume
industry sets great store
by use of the resin,
although nowadays it
is extracted by boiling
up the leaves. It is even
used to give an aroma
to some sweets.

shiny leaf
surface

unstalked

narrow, 4–8cm long

upright growth with
projecting branches

evergreen leaves

Mezereon

Daphne mezereum (mezereon family)
H 0.5–1.2m February–April

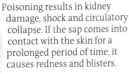

bright red juicy fruit,
0.5–1cm in size

The Mezereon is a highly poisonous, albeit attractive shrub. It can cause a strangling sensation and severe inflammation in the throat. Poisoning results in kidney damage, shock and circulatory collapse. If the sap comes into contact with the skin for a prolonged period of time, it causes redness and blisters.

Habitat *Wild in nearly the whole of Europe in airy woods and on rocky rubble. Grown in small gardens as ornamental tree. Fruit shines brilliant red from among the foliage.*

> *requires slight moisture in soil*
> *flowers have pleasant fragrance*
> *white-flowered variety grown in gardens*

leaves form tufts on tops of twigs

4 dark pink tips, occasionally white

flower up to 1cm across

lanceolate leaf, 3–8cm long

upright growth with thick twigs

short stalk

Bottle-brush

Callistemon sp. (myrtle family)
H 1–4m April–October

numerous stamens, up to more than 3cm long

Indistinctive petals

Above the flower head that resembles a brush used for cleaning out bottles, the twig continues to grow and can develop a new flower the following year. The fruit does not fall from the plant. However fruits remain closed for several years and only open in the heat of bush fires. The resulting ashy surface provides an ideal place for the seeds to germinate.

Habitat *Native to Australia. Grown in gardens in the Mediterranean and as container plants in central Europe. The woody fruit is located directly on the branch.*

> *requires plenty of warmth*
> *some varieties with pink, white or yellow flowers*

cylindrical flower head, rather like a bottle brush

protruding leaves

evergreen leaf, firm and leathery

Myrtle
Myrtus communis (myrtle family)
H 1–5m June–August

Habitat Wild in shrubby areas of the Mediterranean. Grown in central Europe as a tub plant. Flowers situated individually in leaf axils.

> both leaves and flowers with extremely pleasant fragrance
> a small-flowered variety exists for pots
> ancient cultivated plant

According to an old Arabic legend, Adam and Eve took a sprig of Myrtle with them when they were driven out of the Garden of Eden. Throughout history the Myrtle has always been associated with love and in Germany even today, many brides' headdresses are made out of Myrtle leaves as a symbol of love. However, a potted Myrtle plant has a less pleasant superstition attached to it; if it dies, then a death in the household is imminent.

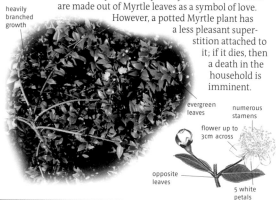

heavily branched growth

evergreen leaves

pointed tip

oval leaf, up to 5cm long

numerous stamens

flower up to 3cm across

opposite leaves

5 white petals

flowers with 4 white petals

Dogwood
Cornus sanguinea (dogwood family)
H 2–5m May–June

Habitat Wild nearly all over Europe in hedgerows, open woods and on woodland edges. Also cultivated. Flowers form flat inflorescences, up to 5cm in width.

> leaves opposite
> dark red branches, especially facing sun
> flowers have unpleasant odour

In former times, this shrub's very hard, tough wood was used in many different ways: it was well-suited for making wooden pegs, pointers, ramrods for rifles, not to mention robust crossbeams for gate locks. The branches provided strong canes to make fences.

bluish-black fruit, up to 8mm in diameter

distinctive dark or purple-red leaves in autumn

widespread growth, often dense

leaf up to 8cm long

3–4, sometimes 5 pairs of curved veins

White Dogwood

Cornus alba (dogwood family)
H 2–4m May–June

As soon as the branches touch the ground, they can develop roots. This is how a dense bush can develop from a single shrub, making it a suitable plant to anchor the soil. In order to control this shrub in gardens, it helps to cut it back regularly. If a leaf is torn apart, thin strands hang off the veins. These are threads which strengthen the water receptacles and are easily extracted.

fruit up to 7mm in diameter, spherical, dirty white to bluish

Habitat *Native to northern Asia. Naturalised in northern Europe, as an ornamental shrub in central Europe. Brilliant red twigs, especially in winter and spring.*

> **leaves opposite**
> **widens with age, also low-lying growth**
> **cultivated in many varieties**

leaf 4–10cm long, pointed tip

underside greyish-green

4–8 pairs of curved veins

181

flower clusters up to 8cm across, with yellowish-white flowers

Did you know?

Varieties of the similar Red Osier Dogwood (Cornus sericea) which originates from the eastern side of North America are distinctive in winter because of their bright yellow-green branches.

leaves can have a white margin

Mountain Laurel

Kalmia latifolia (heather family)

H 0.6–3m May–July

Habitat *Wild in oak and pine forests of the eastern USA. Many garden varieties. Numerous flowers form dense clusters.*

> *evergreen leaves, resembling those of the Bay Laurel (p. 66)*
> *white to purple flowers*
> *extremely poisonous!*

The Mountain Laurel is the state flower of the American states of Pennsylvania and Connecticut. It can reach a height of up to 10m in its natural environment. In gardens it remains a lot smaller and develops its magnificent flowers only on acidic soils in partial shade. In homeopathic dilutions it can ease heart complaints and neuralgia.

broad cup-shaped flower, up to 2.5cm in size

10 stamens

loose form

elliptical leaf, up to 10cm long

shiny green surface

yellowish-green underside

upright branches

Rhododendron hybrids

Rhododendron – hybrid (heather family)

H 0.5–4m May–June

Habitat *Originated from different American and east Asian species. Popular in parks and gardens of Europe. Flowers usually very abundant.*

> *require partial shade*
> *also called 'Japanese Azalea'*
> *varieties have white, pink, lilac or red flowers*

The evergreen rhododendrons which decorate our gardens in their various shapes and colours are the result of much cultivation. They require loose, alkaline-free soils and sufficient air and soil moisture. Therefore they grow especially well in central Europe in coastal areas with sandy or boggy soils.

upper petals often patterned

flower clusters at end of branches

wide, dense growth

broad bell-shaped flower, up to 10cm in size

evergreen leaves

firm, leathery leaf, up to 15cm long

often boat-like, downwards-curved

Alpenrose

Rhododendron ferrugineum (heather family)

H 0.3–1.5m June–July

The Alpenrose grows as an undergrowth shrub in the Alps and prefers moist, acidic soil. Infusion of the leaves in herbal tea causes nausea, a drop in blood pressure, convulsions and cardiac arrest.

5 rounded tips

light-coloured glandular dots

densely branched

brilliant red, bell-shaped flower, about 1.5cm long

Habitat *Wild in the mountainous regions of central and southern Europe on acidic soils up to altitudes of 2,000m and above. Flowers form short clusters at the end of branches.*

> **evergreen leaves**
> **poisonous!**
> **can live up to over 100 years old**

upright to low-lying growth

leathery, sparse leaf about 4cm long

shiny dark green surface

underside with rusty brown scales

183

Hairy Alpenrose

Rhododendron hirsutum (heather family)

H 0.3–1m June–August

Even though alpenroses are well-suited to the raw, cold mountain winters, they still need sufficient snow cover to enable them to develop properly. When planted on lowlands, they are less tolerant of the cold and are often killed by frost. The bushes only grow very slowly, but can reach an age of up to 60 years.

about 1.5cm long

branches curve upwards

bushy growth, densely branched

Habitat *Native to the Alps in dwarf shrubland areas and forests on the tree line. Usually on chalky deposits. Three to 10 flowers packed closely together.*

> **leaves stay green over winter**
> **much less common than the Alpenrose (see above)**
> **protected species**

light red, funnel-shaped bell flowers

leathery leaf, up to 3cm long

margin with many bristles, fringed

Bearberry

Arctostaphylos uva-ursi (heather family)

H 0.2–0.3m April–May

style remnant at tip

brilliant red fruit, 6mm in diameter

Habitat *Wild nearly all over Europe in pine forests and on moorland up to altitudes of around 2,500 m. Fruit remains on the bush until far into the winter season.*

> evergreen leaves
> often forms large crops
> can reach an age of up to 100 years

The Bearberry grows in Europe, Siberia and North America in regions where the constellation of the Great Bear can be viewed (hence the name!). The leaves produce an important component for herbal tea that helps with bladder problems. They disinfect the urine and consequently benefit bladder and urinary tract infections. The tea, however, should not be drunk for longer than a week.

carpet-like growth

jug-shaped flowers, around 0.5cm in size

dark green, glossy surface

light green underside

rough, oval leaf, 1–3cm long

5 pinkish tips

branches lie on ground

Bog Bilberry

Vaccinium uliginosum (heather family)

H 0.2–0.8m May–July

blue, pruinose, spherical or pear-shaped berries

Habitat *Native to Europe on moorlands on wet, acidic soils. Only in mountainous regions in the south. Distinctive because of the bluish leaves.*

> underside of leaves distinctively greyish-green
> fruit contrasts to Blueberry fruit (p. 212), with light-coloured flesh and juice
> often grows in groups

The berries can lead to an intoxicating condition with vomiting. This is caused by a fungus, *Monilinia megalospora*. The fruit of unaffected plants show no signs of infection. As the fungus spores only appear on mummified fruit, it is difficult to tell from its appearance whether or not a fresh berry is infected.

with 4 or occasionally 5 tips

elongated oval flowers, 4–6mm long

alternate leaves, only appear in summer

rough leaf, around 2cm long

rounded tip

bluish-green surface

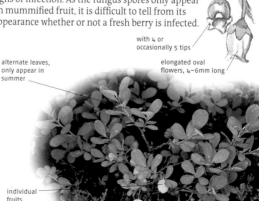

individual fruits

Cowberry

Vaccinium vitis-idaea (heather family)

H 0.1–0.3m May–August

The Swedes describe Cowberry fruit as the 'red gold of the country'. The fruits contain different acids, lots of minerals, vitamin A and C as well as some B vitamins. They can be stored for quite a long time. They do not taste as good when raw, but are very tasty stewed or as a juice. They are best known as an accompaniment to roast venison.

remains of sepals
around tip

red berries

white to light pink
bell-shaped flowers,
4 tips

small dwarf shrub with
densely leaved twigs

Habitat *Wild nearly all over Europe in pine and spruce forests and on moorland. On acidic soils. Grows on moorland often in amongst moss.*

> *evergreen leaves*
> *fruit ripens usually at different intervals*
> *also known as 'Cranberry'*

rough, oval leaf
1–3cm long

margin
slightly
curled over

shiny
surface

spotted
under-
side

185

pendant fruit clusters

Did you know?

*The American Cranberry (*Vaccinium macrocarpon*) grows in North America and has similar uses. Cranberry juice has been a popular, refreshing drink over here for some years now. It is said to ease and prevent urinary tract infections.*

Wild Rosemary

Ledum palustre (heather family)
H 0.5–1.5m May–June

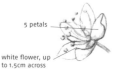

5 petals

white flower, up
to 1.5cm across

Habitat Wild on
pine moors of north
Germany and northern
Europe. On wet, acidic
soils. Flowers on
the end of stems in
distinctive clusters.

> evergreen leaves
> smells like the Camphor
  Laurel (p. 67) when
  crushed
> can lead to kidney dam-
  age if taken by mouth

In Siberia, sprigs were once placed between clothes and also in grain stores to ward off vermin. Large quantities of the fragrant substances contained in the plant have an intoxicating effect. Even the Teutons used the plant as a bitter agent in beer and consequently heightened its intoxicating effect. Right up to the 18th century beer containing Wild Rosemary extract was still available, in spite of its toxic nature.

flowers in clusters
at end of twigs

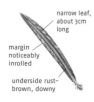

narrow leaf,
about 3cm
long

margin
noticeably
inrolled

underside rust-
brown, downy

upright
branches

Cape Leadwort

Plumbago auriculata (leadwort family)
H 0.5–6m June–September

light blue flowers,
up to 4cm long

5 petal tips

long
tube

Habitat Originates
from South Africa. In
southern Europe in
gardens and grounds,
in central Europe as
container plant. Dis-
tinctive flower clusters,
up to 15cm across.

> flower calyxes extremely
  sticky
> suitable for green
  coverage of pergolas
> also with white flowers

The flowers attract insects with long proboscises, especially moths such as the Hummingbird Hawk-moth (*Macroglossum stellatarum*). The closely related plant Plumbago (*Plumbago europaea*) which grows in the Mediterranean as a footpath and wayside shrub yields a lead grey sap which gave the plant its name.

thin pliant twigs,
often bent over at
the top

leaves mainly
light green

elliptical leaf

wedge-
shaped
at base

short
stalk

Wild Privet
Ligustum vulgare (ash family)
H 2–7m June–July

The Wild Privet tolerates heavy pruning and is therefore suitable as a hedgerow plant. For this purpose, gardeners generally plant the variety 'Atrovirens', as its leaves remain on the branches up until the winter or else do not fall at all. The fruit is often eaten in late winter by birds that ensure the distribution of the undigested seeds they excrete. The fruit was once used to extract a violet colouring for ink.

black berries, up to 1cm in diameter, green inside

Habitat Wild nearly all over Europe in undergrowth and on edges of woodland. Cultivated on banks and in hedgerows. Fruit remains on bush for a long time.

> flowers have unpleasant smell
> tolerates sunshine and partial shade
> all plant parts are poisonous to humans!

4 widely spread petal tips

small white flowers

branches project upwards

dense growth, often irregular

leathery leaf, 2–6cm long

opposite

187

Did you know?
The distinctively coloured caterpillar of the Privet Hawkmoth (Sphinx ligustri) occasionally feeds on the bush. This is the largest species of moth found in Britain.

Lilac

Syringa vulgaris (ash family)
H 2–6m April–May

Habitat *Native to south-eastern Europe on rocky slopes and in woods. In central Europe in parks and gardens. Flowers in dense clusters.*

> *grows in almost every farmyard garden*
> *flowers have very intense fragrance*
> *flower colours range from white to deep purple*

In the 16th century the first Lilac branch was brought from Constantinople to Vienna and from there it was taken to the whole of central Europe. Although it was not until the 19th century that intensive cultivation began, there are now about 900 different varieties. In some countries the fragrant essential oil is used for perfumes. In Germany, Lilac soap was particularly enjoyed in a luxurious bath.

opens with 2 flaps

leathery fruit capsule

corolla tube up to 1.5cm long

4 widely spread petal tips

wedge or heart-shaped base

opposite

oval leaf, 5–12cm long

flower clusters at end of branches

branches straight upright

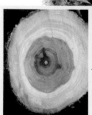

Did you know?
The centre of the very hard Lilac wood is tinged with a violet colour, at least when fresh. It is suitable for turning and polishes up really well to a glossy finish.

Duke of Argyll's Teaplant

Lycium barbarum (nightshade family)
H 2–3m May–September

The Duke of Argyll's Teaplant can tolerate urban air, salt, dryness, wind and heat. This is why it is suitable for green coverage along roadsides. Its thin twigs often grow into other shrubs and then form an impenetrable tangle. Even if it is cut down to ground level, the shrub usually grows back rapidly.

5 petal tips

purple to violet flower, around 1cm long

thin twigs

very variable leaf form

Habitat Native to China. Introduced to southern and central Europe. Planted on streets and walls. Fruit usually abundant.

> **leaf form very variable**
> **tolerates salty soil**
> **poisonous!**

greyish-green leaf, up to 6cm long

red oval berries, up to 2cm long

Angel's Trumpet

Brugmansia varieties (nightshade family)
H 1–3m June–October

Any contact with this plant's sap may cause poisoning. In large quantities, it can lead to severe intoxication and radically alter a person's mental state. The use of the plant as a narcotic is usually fatal. Native South Americans used Angel's Trumpet to make contact with ghosts of their ancestors.

funnel-shaped flower, up to 30cm long

5 tips

suspended flowers

strong branches

large leaves

Habitat Originates from South America. In southern Europe in gardens and in central Europe as a container plant. Very characteristic large folded trumpet flowers.

> **leaf margins entire or roughly serrated**
> **fragrant flowers at night**
> **varieties with different flower colours**

soft leaf, up to 25cm long

Oleander

Nerium oleander (dogbane family)
H 1–4m July–September

many varieties
have dense or
double flowers

The flowers are particularly fragrant in the evening and attract night time butterflies. In the south the Oleander Hawk-moth (*Daphnis nerii*) probes the flowers for nectar with its long proboscis. The bush contains elements that can stimulate the heart, with fatal consequences if the dose is large. The leaves also act as effective poison against mice and rats.

Habitat Wild in the Mediterranean along riverbanks, by edges of streams and planted along motorways. As container plants in central Europe. Flowers range from white to deep red.

> without leaves bears some resemblance to a willow
> resistant to exhaust fumes
> highly poisonous!

leathery leaves, up to 15cm long

underside lighter in colour

distinctive central vein

spindle-like fruit, up to 10cm long

flowers about 5cm across

5 petal tips with fringes

evergreen leaves

growth rigidly upright

190

Did you know?

The ripe fruits burst open, releasing distinctive, long-haired seeds. In dry weather these are dispersed by the wind, in wet weather they become attached to passing grazing animals.

Alternate-leaved Butterfly Bush

Buddleja alternifolia (butterfly-bush family)
H 2–4m June

In contrast to the Butterfly Bush (p. 214), the leaves of this bush are alternate. This prolific flowering tree is also hardy in central Europe and is suitable as an individual plant on sunny terraces or on lawned areas.

flowering branches hang in cascades

4 petal tips

purple–lilac flowers up to 1.3cm wide

long corolla tubes

Habitat *Originates from China. In Europe as ornamental shrub in gardens. Flowers in dense, abundant clusters along branches*

> *rapid growing*
> *flowers smell tangy*
> *undersides of leaves downy*

slender leaf, up to 10cm long

pointed tip

Common Thyme

Thymus vulgaris (dead-nettle family)
H 0.1–0.3m April–June

The Greeks of the Ancient World used to burn Common Thyme in sacrificial fires. This is the origin of the plant's name: Greek 'thyein' means 'to smoke'. The plant contains an essential oil that acts as a disinfectant. Even the ancient Egyptians were familiar with this effect. They treated wounds with thyme and also used the oils in the process of mummification.

Habitat *Wild in the western Mediterranean. In sunny, dry locations. Planted as an herb. Also an ornamental plant due to its lovely flowers.*

> *characteristic aroma*
> *often cultivated as a healing and herbal plant*
> *also hardy in central Europe*

dense dwarf shrub

deep 3-part lower lip

white to pinkish lipped flowers 4–6mm long

flowers in thick clusters

opposite leaves, under 1cm long

underside white, downy

rolled-up margin

Dwarf Honeysuckle
Lonicera xylosteum (honeysuckle family)
H 1–3m May–June

Habitat *Wild in central Europe in shrubberies and on woodland edges. Planted in gardens and parks. Characteristic red fruits arranged in pairs.*

> grows in full shade or partial shade
> leaves emerge early
> poisonous fruit! Can cause sickness and palpitations

Gardeners occasionally used to plant this shrub as a hedge plant around gardens and estate grounds. It is particularly unsuitable for playground areas though, as children can be attracted to the red berries which are poisonous. The name *xylosteum* means 'rock hard wood' and refers to the extremely hard wood which cracks loudly when the twigs snap.

broad elliptical leaf, up to 6cm long

opposite

usually soft hairs on both sides

densely branched

growth wide-spreading and upright

crown 1–1.5cm long, initially white, later light yellow

2 flowers shared on each stalk

berries adjacent, in pairs

shiny red berries, about 0.5cm thick

Dwarf Alpine Honeysuckle
Lonicera alpigena (honeysuckle family)
H 1–2m May–June

Habitat *Wild on alkaline soils in mountainous regions of central and southern Europe. The 2 fruits grow together into one large double fruit.*

> opposite leaves
> twigs hollow inside
> occasionally grows as ornamental shrub in gardens

The Dwarf Alpine Honeysuckle grows not only in the Alps but also in forest woodlands of other mountainous regions. The honeysuckles bear the name *Lonicera* in honour of the German doctor and botanist Adam Lonitzer, who lived in the 16th century and whose botanical books include a key herbal and also a work on natural history.

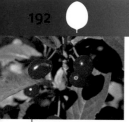

oval, elongated leaf, up to 10cm long

2-lipped flowers, always in pairs

fruits in leaf axils

dull red exterior

shiny dark green surface

lighter underside

straight upright growth

Leatherleaf Viburnum

Viburnum rhytidophyllum (honeysuckle family)

H 3–5m May–June

The Leatherleaf Viburnum is very popular with gardeners, because it is extremely robust. Additionally, with its evergreen leaves and long lasting rich attractive fruit the plant is very decorative. The fruit is inedible for humans and is only eaten by birds during the course of the winter, when more tasty nourishment is scarce.

felt-like stalk with hairs

elliptical fruit, around 8mm long, shiny black when ripe

Habitat *Native to central and western China. In Europe in gardens, parks and grounds. Abundant fruit is initially brilliant red.*

> *leaf underside dense grey – or yellowish, downy*
> *evergreen leaves*
> *very hardy, frost resistant*

oval elongated leaf, 8–20cm long

dark green, heavily wrinkled

Did you know?

The flower buds withstand the cold throughout winter, with only a hairy felt to protect them for next year. In severe frost the leaves often point downwards and straighten up again in warmer weather.

compact growth, though frequently quite irregular

many upright, fairly rigid branches

Common Snowberry

Symphoricarpos albus (honeysuckle family)
H 1.5–2m June–September

Habitat *Originates from North America. In Europe in gardens, parks and on embankments. Unmistakeable due to snowball-like fruit.*

> berries can cause vomiting or diarrhoea
> often with rough lobed leaves
> flowers attract bees

The berries of this bush are given different nicknames in Germany, depending on the region. If they are thrown onto the ground with force or trodden upon, they burst open with a more or less loud crack. The spongy fruit flesh does not contain any white colouring but completely reflects the light as it falls.

fruit densely packed together

thin twigs

pink bell-shaped flowers, about 5mm long

leaf elliptical to roundish, about 5cm long

dark green surface

bluish-green underside

opposite leaves

white spherical fruit, 1–1.5cm in size, easily crushed

194

Butcher's Broom

Ruscus aculeatus (lily family)
H 0.2–0.9m February–April

tiny flowers

sessile, flat shoots

Habitat *Wild in the Mediterranean and in copses and woodlands of western Europe. Rarely in gardens. Produces flowers and fruit directly on the leaves.*

> impenetrable wood
> male and female plants
> branches suitable for dried flower and fruit arrangements

The spiky branches of the Butcher's Broom at one time successfully prevented mice from pillaging when they were placed lying down or hanging up between stores of food. The rigid twigs also produced durable brooms. Nowadays the Butcher's Broom plays a significant part as a healing plant for the treatment of vascular problems.

spherical fruit, up to 8mm in diameter

evergreen

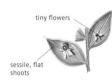

often with dead branches

flat leafy shoot

up to 3cm long

spiky tip

stiff branches

broad, bushy

Bog-myrtle

Myrica gale (bog-myrtle family)
H 0.5–1.5m April–May

The Vikings used the aromatic, albeit poisonous Bog-myrtle to flavour beer. The brew had a severely inebriating effect and could also cause fits of rage. Old herbal books recommend the leaves of the Bog-myrtle to help induce abortion and control vermin.

Habitat *Wild in western and central Europe on wetland and moorland. Cultivated by pond edges. Small fruit in thick catkins.*

> *pleasant aroma when crushed*
> *male and female shrubs*
> *wild shrubs are a protected species in parts of Britain*

female catkins turn brownish after flowering

yellow stamens

male flower catkin, about 1cm long

female flower catkin, about 0.5cm long

alternate leaves emerging only after first flowering

leaf 2–5cm long, with resinous glands

roughly serrated at top only

Grey Sallow

Salix cinerea (willow family)
H 2–5m April–May

The flowery twigs of the Grey Sallow resemble at first glance those of the Goat Willow (p. 80). However the broad form of the shrub and the grey felt on its branches and leaves are good indicators. The bush can tolerate its base being in water for a long time. It is therefore one of the trees that grows closest to the water on riverbanks.

Habitat *Wild nearly all over Europe on moorland, in bogs, ditches, on banks of streams and by lakes. Even inconspicuous female flowers attract bees.*

> *anthers mainly orangey-red in flowering season*
> *young twigs have grey, downy hairs*
> *also known as 'Grey Willow'*

male flowers in catkins up to 4cm long before foliage appears

very broad form, often almost semi-circular

densely branched

grey-green leaf, 3–10cm long, irregularly toothed

underside soft, with light grey hairs

Purple Willow
Salix purpurea (willow family)
H 2–6m March–April

Habitat *Wild in western, southern and central Europe by rivers, in riverside glades and gravel pits. Especially characteristic red anthers appear before blossom.*

> flowers appear before foliage
> one of the most common willows
> also planted as spreading variety and to keep soil firm and compact

narrow lanceolate leaves, 4–12cm long

dull dark green surface

hairless bluish-green underside

Even herbalists of the Ancient World used willow bark to counteract pain and fever. The reason for this is the element salicin that is found in abundance even in the Purple Willow. Today, salicin is still used in herbal teas to help control high temperatures and rheumatic pain. Nowadays, man-made variations of salicin, such as acetylene salicinic acid, are more important than the bark itself.

flowers in 2–5cm long slender catkins

branches thin but firm

richly and densely branched

anthers red before opening

very variable form, often irregular

Olive Willow
Salix elaeagnos (willow family)
H 3–6m April–May

Habitat *Wild in mountainous regions of central and southern Europe. Frequently planted. Forms abundant catkins either before or with the foliage.*

> leaf form vaguely resembles Lavender leaf
> can also grow on drained soils
> golden-yellow autumn foliage

toothed margin, often curled under

leaf up to 20cm long, around 1cm wide

underside with dense felt-like hairs

The Olive Willow often forms dense colonies on gravel surfaces by mountain streams and rivers. It appears as one of the first trees in such locations and helps to anchor the soil. For this reason the tree is also planted near gravel pits and on scree slopes. Due to its abundant and early flowering it has found its way into parks and grounds as an ornamental bush.

upright branches with forked twigs

narrow yellow flower catkins, usually crooked

Green Alder

Alnus viridis (birch family)
H 1–3m April–June

The Green Alder is found on shady slopes above the Alpine tree line and is regarded as a natural pioneer tree to colonise slippery mountain slopes and stabilise avalanche debris. Planted as a protective tree it can prevent erosion and avalanches and facilitates reforestation with other trees.

Habitat *Mountain tree of central and southern Europe. Prolific growth particularly above tree line.*

> **broad form, often low lying**
> **tolerates long periods of snow cover**
> **also known as 'Mountain Alder'**

pendant male flower catkins up to 7cm long

cone-like fruit stalks up to 1.3cm long

upright female flower catkins

oval to circular leaf, 3–8cm long

pointed tip

irregularly serrated margin

Shrubby Birch

Betula humilis (birch family)
H 0.5–2m April–May

In central Europe the Shrubby Birch is a rare survivor of the last Ice Age. Large crops of this tree grow in northern Europe and Siberia. The shrub tolerates severe frost and manages well with its short growth period. The similar Dwarf Birch in the north remains smaller and has leaves of up to 1.5cm.

Habitat *Wild from north-eastern Europe to southern Germany. Oval fruit catkins are usually in an upright position.*

> **requires wet soils**
> **pioneer tree**
> **grows only on moorland in central Europe**

branches with white warty glands

male flower catkins in upright position, up to 1.5cm long

pointed leaf, longer than width, 1–3.5cm long

irregularly serrated margin

Hazel
Corylus avellana (birch family)
H 2–7m February–April

Habitat *Wild all over Europe in deciduous forests, on edges of woods and in hedgerows. Planted in gardens and parks. Fruit ripens from September onwards.*

> **sometimes even flowers in December**
> **pollen carried on the wind**
> **can trigger allergies**

Hazelnuts contain a lot of fatty oil, protein and vitamins and minerals. The shrub used to be a valuable source of nutrition for the Celts and the Vikings. It was also said to ward off witches and evil spirits. Nowadays its flexible 'sticks' are used in the production of walking sticks and divining rods as well as wicker material for basket makers. Commercially sold hazelnuts are usually the larger fruits of the southern European Filbert (*Corylus maxima*).

female flowers hidden in a bud

male flowers hang in catkins up to 10cm long

oval, roundish or heart-shaped leaf, 5–10cm long

with soft hairs

double-toothed margin

flowers long before foliage appears

brown hazelnuts

tubular or bell-shaped involucre

Did you know?
Contrary to the growth pattern of other plants, the commonly cultivated Corkscrew Hazel (Corylus avellana 'contorta') grows in the direction of gravity. The branches therefore grow in a twisted and contorted fashion.

usually many straight upright branches

Kermes Oak

Quercus coccifera (beech family)
H 0.5–4m March–May

Kermes scale insects feed off the Kermes Oak. These white pea-sized creatures contain a red fluid, from which a crimson colouring can be extracted. The extraction process diminished severely, however, in the 19th century, as the cochineal scale insects bred on the Prickly Pear (p. 165) were able to produce a substantial additional amount of colouring.

mainly bushy form

densely branched

acorn up to 3cm long

cupule with prickly scales

Habitat From the Mediterranean to higher locations, on scrubland and in forests. Fruits which ripen in the second year are often larger than the foliage.

> evergreen leaves
> leaves resemble those of the English Holly (p. 115)
> if not damaged by goats or fires it would grow into a tree shape

tough, leathery leaf, 1.5–4cm long

indented wavy margin with spiky teeth

Wintergreen Barberry

Berberis julianae (barberry family)
H 2–3m May–June

There are almost 500 different types of barberry, many of which are grown in gardens as ornamental shrubs. Wintergreen Barberry is one of the most commonly planted, extremely robust varieties. The name 'barberry' is linked to the Berbers, possibly because many varieties were introduced into Europe from the Far East.

upright growth, very heavily branched

bluish-black, acutely pruinose

berries 7–8mm long

Habitat Originates from China. In Europe In gardens, grounds and parks. Evergreen, though older leaves turn different colours in autumn.

> evergreen leaves
> can be pruned in the same way as hedges
> poisonous!

tough, leathery leaf, 5–9cm long

margin with serrated teeth

light green underside

1–4cm long thorn with 3 parts

Common Barberry
Berberis vulgaris (barberry family)
H 2–3m May–June

Habitat *Wild in central and southern Europe on woodland edges, in hedgerows and copses. Planted as an ornamental shrub. Berries in hanging clusters.*

> requires warmth in summer
> good shrub to encourage birds
> poisonous except for ripened fruit!

In contrast to most other varieties of barberry, the ripened fruit of the Common Barberry is edible. The fruit does taste sour, however, as it contains fruit acids. Poor people at one time pressed out the juices to use instead of vinegar. Nowadays the dried fruit is for sale in Turkish shops and market stalls as an acidic cooking ingredient and also for refreshing fruit teas.

thorns with mainly 3 parts

tough leaf, 2–6cm long

margin with prickly teeth

clusters with many yellow flowers

irregular form, upright or broad, mainly squarrose

elliptical red berries, about 1cm long

Did you know?
The bark contains yellow substances that can be used to dye wool, leather, cotton and silk in different shades of yellow. Extracts from the bark are often found in drugs for the gall bladder and for liver complaints as well as rheumatism.

Camellia

Camellia japonica (camellia family)
H 2–10m January–April

In Japan and China the Camellia is one of the most important evergreen decorative garden shrubs and is also popular in southern Europe. The closely related Teaplant (*Camellia sinensis*) on the other hand is a plant with a significant economic purpose: its fermented or dried green leaves produce a stimulating black or green tea.

Habitat *Wild, native to Japan. Many cultivated varieties. In southern Europe in gardens and as pot plant in central Europe. Many varieties produce full or double flowers.*

> **upright or projectile growth**
> **requires plenty of warmth**
> **varieties exist with different coloured flowers**

abundant stamens

flowers up to more than 10cm in size

flowers mainly solitary

evergreen leaves

stiff, leathery leaf, 5–10cm long

shiny dark green surface

toothed margin

Buttercup Winterhazel

Corylopsis pauciflora (witch-hazel family)
H 1–1.5m March–April

The leaves of this shrub and also its light yellow flower clusters are said to bear some resemblance to those of the Hazel (p. 198). However this can only be said of the flowers when they are observed from a distance. On the Buttercup Winterhazel, the petals are distinctly yellow, whereas on the Hazel, the stamens produce this conspicuous yellow colour.

Habitat *Native to mountains of Japan. In Europe as an ornamental garden shrub. Flowers appear before foliage.*

> **flowers remain lovely over a long period of time**
> **leaves turn yellow in autumn**

broad bushy form

fragrant, light yellow bell-shaped flowers

5 petals

numerous dense and fine branches

oval to heart-shaped leaf, up to 7cm long

margin with bristly teeth

Hybrid Witch Hazel
Hamamelis x *intermedia* (witch-hazel family)
H 3–5m December–March

Habitat *Only known as cultivated shrub. Different varieties cultivated in gardens and parks. Flowers in very early spring, long before foliage emerges.*

> leaves resemble those of the Hazel (p. 198)
> petals curl up in cold weather
> can flower for several weeks

The first varieties of the Hybrid Witch Hazel originated at the beginning of the 20th century in Belgium. This was a result of a cross between the Japanese Witchhazel (*Hamamelis japonica*) and the Chinese Witchhazel (*Hamamelis chinensis*). The enchanting characteristic of this tree is that it flowers in winter, often in the middle of the snowy season. The flowers can resist temperatures of −10 degrees Celsius without becoming damaged. The ripened fruit opens in an explosive motion, flinging out the seeds.

4 narrow strap-like petals, up to 2cm long

4 sepals

leaf 10–15cm long, often asymmetrical

rough surface

toothed margin with irregular indentations

long, slanted, projectile branches

upright growth

202

red petals on some varieties

woody fruit

Did you know?
*The flowers of the Virginia Witchhazel (*Hamamelis virginiana*), which comes from the eastern part of North America, emerge in autumn when the leaves fall. Extracts from its leaves and bark can help counteract various skin problems.*

Bigleaf Hydrangea

Hydrangea macrophylla (mockorange family)
H 1–1.5m July–September

The flower colour can vary depending on the variety: if you buy a blue variety in the nursery, the balls of flowers may be pink the following year. This indicates that the plant lacks the aluminium required to produce the blue colour. Special hydrangea fertilisers or potash alum in the spring as well as rainwater or water containing vinegar can solve the problem.

variety with fertile central flowers

flowers on edge are sterile

Habitat *Originates from Japan and Korea. Found as pot plant varieties, in cemeteries and gardens. Different coloured flowers can be found on one single stem.*

> *flowers can be white, pink or blue*
> *requires sufficiently moist soil*
> *often dies back in winter*

4 distinctive sepals

8 anthers

4 small petals

flowers domed to ball-shaped, up to 20cm in size

mainly broad, almost spherical growth

oval, thick leaf up to 20cm long

underside lighter

roughly serrated margin

203

Fuzzy Pride-of-Rochester

Deutzia scabra (mockorange family)
H 2–3m May–June

There are many kinds of garden varieties of Fuzzy Pride-of-Rochester. All are easily recognised by their undemanding nature and distinctive, prolific flowers. They are very easy and quick to propagate as well as easily transplanted so they are marketed in tree nurseries at very reasonable prices.

flower bell to star shaped, up to 2cm wide

Habitat *Wild form is originally native to Japan. Varieties found in Europe in gardens, parks and grounds. Leaves can appear lightly spotted.*

> *opposite leaves*
> *flowers smell like honey*
> *varieties also exist with double flowers*

branches and flower clusters more or less pendent or hanging

upright growth

oval, pointed leaf, 3–8cm long

both sides very rough

finely serrated margin

Fragrant Mockorange

Philadelphus coronarius (mockorange family)
H 1–3m May–June

Habitat *Wild especially in the eastern Mediterranean and in Asia Minor. In gardens and parks of central Europe. Distinctive flowers in groups of 5–9.*

> flowers have very fragrant scent
> undemanding, frost resistant, widespread ornamental shrub
> also called 'Sweet Mockorange'

As the flowers of the Fragrant Mockorange smell very strongly of jasmine, it is often mistaken for True Jasmine (see box). Although its flowers do not produce fragrance for the perfume industry, a blossoming branch can nevertheless bring the beguiling fragrance indoors. Recorders were once made out of the branches. In the 18th century the shafts of tobacco pipes were also manufactured from them.

fruit capsule with 4 flaps

withered sepal

pointed tip

pointed toothed margin

leaf up to 9cm long

204

flowers up to 3.5cm wide

4 flat creamy white wide-opened petals

upright growth, branches often overhanging

Did you know?

*The True Jasmine (*Jasminum officinale*) is a climbing shrub from Asia, which has been cultivated in Europe. Its flowers produce fragrance for perfumes. In central Europe it is only cultivated in containers, as it is not hardy enough to survive the winter.*

Japanese Meadowsweet

Spiraea japonica (rose family)
H 0.3–0.6m June–July

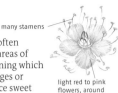

many stamens

These low-maintenance bushes are often planted close together to give large areas of green coverage. They withstand pruning which makes them well-suited also for hedges or roadside borders. The flowers produce sweet nectar and consequently attract masses of wild bees, flies and beetles.

light red to pink flowers, around 0.5cm across

Habitat Wild, native to Japan. Cultivated varieties in Europe in parks and gardens. Flowers form dense, umbrella-like clusters.

> can also have white flowers
> very popular as summer blossoming shrub
> easy to maintain

rigid upright branches, sparsely twigged

dense form

oval–lanceolate leaf

single to double serrated margin

Bridal Wreath

Spiraea x vanhouttei (rose family)
H 2–3m May–June

Amongst the white-flowering spiraeas, there is a huge range of similar types and varieties, which are a wonderful adornment for every garden.
Theophrastos, an ancient Greek philosopher, mentions 'speiraia' as a shrub used for garlands. This name is really well-suited for the *Spiraea* with its long, prolific flowering branches.

Habitat In 1862, the Belgian horticulturalist, Louis van Houtte, first cultivated the plant from an ornamental shrub. Often in gardens, parks and estate grounds. Distinctive due to its abundant flowers.

> requires sunny locations
> flowering branches ideal for bouquets
> also known as 'Van Houtte's Spiraea'

dense form

5 white petals

long branches, bending upwards, more or less overhanging

leaf 3–5cm long, roughly serrated, tip almost lobed

many stamens

flowers 0.8cm wide

bluish–green underside

European Serviceberry

Amelanchier ovalis (rose family)
H 1–3m April–May

elongated petals

flowers up to 2.5cm across

Habitat *Wild in southern and central Europe on rocks, rubble and in sunny, dry forests. Flowers in groups of 3 to 6.*

> **often with prolific flowering**
> **young leaves initially white, downy, bare later on**
> **fruit less aromatic than species below**

The bush pushes its roots deep into crevices and manages to find sufficient moisture even on seemingly dry rocks. It is known in Upper Bavaria in Germany as the 'Edelweiss tree' because of its white downy leaves. The fruit was at one time used as a substitute for currants and raisins.

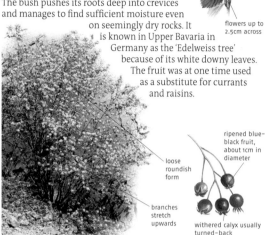

oval-shaped leaf, 2–4cm long

heavily serrated margin

ripened blue-black fruit, about 1cm in diameter

loose roundish form

branches stretch upwards

withered calyx usually turned-back

June Berry

Amelanchier lamarckii (rose family)
H 6–8m May

5 white, elongated petals, up to 1.5cm long

Habitat *Native to eastern North America. In parks and gardens of Europe, also wild. Leaves turn orange to red in autumn.*

> **emerging leaves tinged with copper red**
> **flower clusters with 8–10 flowers**
> **fruit attracts birds**

The June Berry is normally grown in gardens as an ornamental shrub. However, the tree produces delicious, sweet fruit, which smells similar to the Bilberry (p. 212). The ripe black fruits are ideal for making jam, jellies or liqueur. However, chewing the seeds of unripe fruit can lead to gastric problems.

crown wide-spreading

broad, sturdy form

fruit up to 1cm in diameter

whitish underside with silky hairs

elliptical leaf, 4–8cm long

protruding withered calyx

Chinese Quince

Chaenomeles sp. (rose family)
H 0.5–3m March–April

The first Chinese Quince shrubs arrived in Europe at the end of the 18th century. Since then, cultivators have favoured this tree with its lovely flowers, and it has quickly become a widespread undemanding, decorative shrub. The hard fruits have a very pleasant smell, which is why housewives used to place them in the linen cupboard. They are also ideal ingredients for making jams and jellies.

flowers often red, but also white, pink or orange

5 petals

abundant stamens

Habitat *Originates from eastern Asia. Many different varieties in gardens and parks of Europe. Fruit bears some resemblance to the Quince (p. 68).*

> *often flowers again in autumn*
> *fruit ripens from September to November*
> *many different varieties*

2 large stipules

oval to elongated leaf, up to 12cm long

usually with rigid thorns

207

profusion of flowers in groups along twigs

Did you know?

Quince plantations are especially common in Latvia where the fruit is produced on a large scale. The fruit is popularly known as the 'Lemon of the North' and the juice that is extracted is a rich source of Vitamin C and often used as lemon juice.

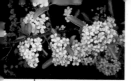

Scarlet Firethorn
Pyracantha coccinea (rose family)
H 1–3m May–June

Habitat *Natural form in southern Europe. In central Europe in domestic gardens, parks, on roadsides, for hedges. Masses of flowers are formed, about 8mm in size.*

> *takes its name from fruit's brilliant colour*
> *leaves usually do not fall until spring*
> *good nesting shrub for birds*

As well as its thorns, this attractive shrub unfortunately suffers a further disadvantage: it very frequently falls victim to fire blight, a dangerous bacterial disease occurring in different members of the rose family and leading to massive losses in the fruit-growing industry. Affected bushes have withered branches bearing dried-up blackish-brown leaves and fruit.

squarrose growth, densely branched

usually flowers abundantly

leathery leaf, up to 4cm long

shiny surface

margin finely serrated

flower's withered remnants

orange to red fruit, 5–6mm in size

208

Japanese Rose
Kerria japonica (rose family)
H 1–2m May–June

Habitat *Originates from deciduous forests of central and southern China. In gardens, parks and grounds of Europe. Double flowers reminiscent of small roses.*

> *wild form rare*
> *undemanding*
> *also called 'Jew's Mallow', (variety with double flowers only)*

The Japanese Rose was already growing in Chinese gardens long before it arrived on our shores. This is also where the dense or double flowered variety originated, which was introduced into Europe at the beginning of the 19th century and from then on very quickly became widespread. The original variety with single flowers is cultivated considerably less.

5 brilliant yellow petals

flower 3cm in size

profusion of stamens

branches often bent over

dense bushy growth

leaf with pointed tip

doubly serrated margin

oval, 3–6cm long

2 small stipules

Blackthorn

Prunus spinosa (rose family)
H 1–3m March–April

white flowers, up to
1.5cm across

5 petals

In comparison to the Whitethorn (p. 221), the
Blackthorn gets its name from the dark-coloured bark of its
branches. This tree provides birds with important protection and
nesting places. In winter, its fruit remains on the branches for a
long time and is food for birds and mammals.

Habitat Grows in the
wild all over Europe on
woodland edges and
in sunny hedgerows.
When ripe, the berries
are first blue, then
blackish-blue.

> *flowers appear mainly
  individually, less
  commonly in pairs*
> *flowers emerge before
  foliage*
> *after first frost, fruit
  tastes less sharp*

acutely squarrose
and dense form

produces impenetrable
undergrowth

spherical fruit, up to
1.5cm in diameter

lanceolate
leaf, up to
5cm long

serrated
margin

masses of
hard, sharp
thorns

dark green
surface

Christ's Thorn

Paliurus spina-cristi (buckthorn family)
H 2–3m May–September

1 straight and 1
crooked thorn at
every leaf node

Despite the fact that the branches are extremely
thorny, they were probably not used to
compose the crown of thorns worn by Christ.
Scientists believe that the Thorny Burnett
(*Sarcopoterium spinosum*) was used;
this is a member of the rose family
commonly found in Israel. The name
'Christ's Thorn' is used for various
thorny plants.

Habitat Wild in the
Mediterranean in
copses, forest margins.
Easily distinguishable
by its characteristic
fruit.

> *flowers attract many
  insects*
> *fruit remains on bush
  throughout winter*
> *tolerates dryness*

fruit with 2–2.5cm
lampshade-like wings

many small yellowish flowers

thorny twigs in characteristic
zigzag formation

leaf mainly slanted oval,
up to 5cm long

3 lengthwise
veins

margin
crenate

European Spindletree

Euonymus europaea (spindle family)
H 1.5–3m May

Habitat *Wild nearly all over Europe in hedgerows, riverside woodlands, along stream banks. Fruit especially distinctive.*

> opposite leaves
> autumn colouring orange to brilliant red
> poisonous!

The fruit of the European Spindletree is reminiscent of a mitre, the head covering of priests. At one time wood turners produced knitting needles, wooden pegs and yarn spindles from the hard, resilient, very durable timber. This is how the tree got its name. It is also good for producing charcoal.

Did you know?

In late spring, frequently the shrub is stripped bare of foliage and criss-crossed with webs. These are home to groups of Spindle Ermine larvae, which pupate here. Around July time, white moths with black spots hatch out.

leaf up to 8cm long

margin serrated crenate

squarrose upright form, with single or multiple stems

210

4 narrow, greenish-yellow to whitish petals

flowers up to 1cm in size

pink to purple fruit, up to 1.5cm across

opens with 4 flaps

seeds with orange coloured coat

Spotted Laurel

Aucuba japonica (dogwood family)
H 2–2.5m March–April

stone fruit 1–1.5cm long

shiny red

The Spotted Laurel used to be seen frequently as an everlasting, decorative plant in butchers' shop windows. The varieties with speckled leaves are particularly popular as ornamental shrubs. It thrives well in central Europe in plant containers, especially placed in cool stairwells and conservatories.

Habitat *Wild in China, Japan and Korea. In parks and gardens of southern Europe, pot plant in central Europe. Fruit remains attached to shrub over winter.*

rigid form, dense and bushy, often almost spherical

> *evergreen leaves, leathery*
> *flowers very indistinct*
> *tolerates shady locations*

margin with a few rough teeth

shiny green surface, often with light flecks

opposite leaves

Alpine Bearberry

Arctostaphylos alpina (heather family)
H 0.1–0.3m May

spherical flowers, about 5mm in size

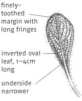

Dairymen working in some Swiss Alpine pastures used to quench their thirst by consuming the ripe, tangy-tasting fruit of the Alpine Bearberry. In other areas, however, the berries were wrongly regarded as being poisonous. This small shrub grows in the Alps, often in the same location and together with another family member, the Bearberry (p. 184).

Habitat *Native to the Arctic and high mountainous regions of Europe. Flowers emerge in spring with leaves.*

> *fruit only ripens in the year after it flowers*
> *requires damp soil*
> *suitable for rockeries*

conspicuous red autumn foliage

shiny blue–black ripe fruit, 6mm in diameter

finely-toothed margin with long fringes

inverted oval leaf, 1–4cm long

underside narrower

dwarf shrub with low-lying branches

Bilberry

Vaccinium myrtillus (heather family)

H 0.15–0.5m April–June

Habitat Wild in northern and central Europe and in mountainous regions of southern Europe. In forests, on moorland heaths. Often grows extensively.

> twigs distinctively irregular
> important forest fruit
> also called 'Blueberry'

Delicious-tasting Bilberries contain fruit acids, valuable minerals and vitamins. Fresh Bilberries act more as a laxative, whereas dried ones and Bilberry juice alleviate diarrhoea. If you pick the fruit, you will no doubt be familiar with the stubborn stain it leaves on fingers as well as clothes. The fruit was once used for dying wool and colouring playing cards and wine.

spherical blue–black berry, bluish-red inside with dark coloured juice

roundish oval, more or less pointed

leaf up to 3cm long

spherical flower, 4–7mm long, greenish to pale pink in colour or tinged purple

Did you know?

The many varieties of cultivated blueberries originate from the North American Blueberry (Vaccinium corymbosum). This produces shrubs up to 2m tall and berries with colourless flesh and juice.

212

dwarf shrub with protruding green twigs

densely leafed

alternate leaves

Forsythia

Forsythia sp. (ash family)
H 2–3m April–May

fruit with 2
flaps, rarely
developed

The magnificent early flowering of the Forsythia delights most garden lovers. Although it contains sugar-rich nectar and
flower up
to 5cm in size
pollen rich with protein, honeybees and wild bees almost never visit it. The reason for this is still unknown. In naturalised gardens it is usually good advice to abandon the Forsythia and plant members of the willow family, for example, instead.

corolla with 4 tips

branches
upright to
overhanging

densely
branched growth

Habitat Natural form in eastern Asia. Ornamental shrub in sunny locations in Europe over the last 100 years. Flowers emerge before leaves.

> radiant eye-catcher in spring gardens
> propagates through cuttings
> many varieties with light to dark yellow flowers

serrated
margin at
least in upper
section

oval to
lanceolate
leaf

False Olive

Phillyrea angustifolia (ash family)
H 1–3m May–June

The False Olive is closely related to the Olive Tree (p. 79). Its small fruits produce plentiful fruit flesh around their hard stone. They hold no interest for humans but birds and small mammals enjoy eating them and, in doing so, distribute the seeds via their excrement.

dense,
squarrose
form

blue-black fruit, up to
1cm in diameter

pointed tip
due to
attached style

Habitat In Mediterranean from Spain to Croatia in shrubbery and open forests. Leaf axils contain multiple, aromatic fruits.

> evergreen
> can also develop leaves with smooth margin
> leaves often conspicuously protruding upwards

lightly
serrated
margin

narrow
lanceolate leaf

Royal Red Butterfly-bush
Buddleja davidii (butterfly-bush family)
H 3–4m July–September

Habitat Originates from the mountains in western China. Ornamental shrub in gardens and parks, wasteland, on station embankments. Flowers also white or pink.

> flowers smell strongly aromatic, especially in evening
> arrived in Europe around 1900

In the whole range of new varieties of this bush, cultivators place as much importance on hardiness as on richness of flowering and flower colour. The reason is that in cold European winters the bush can completely freeze to death. However it does usually develop new shoots again at its base. The extremely lightweight seeds are dispersed by the wind and can become attached to passing vehicles. As a result, the bush can be found growing in desolate urban areas, on station embankments, street verges and in industrial areas.

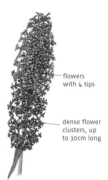

flowers with 4 tips

dense flower clusters, up to 30cm long

margin with small forwards–directed teeth

white downy underside

lanceolate leaf, up to 25cm long

growth often spherical

214

flower clusters at end of annual germination

numerous little upright stems

Did you know?
The flowers produce abundant nectar and are visited by masses of insects, especially butterflies. The diversity of species of butterflies is not increased, however, as this mainly depends on the plants which the caterpillars feed on.

Beauty Berry
Callicarpa bodinieri (verbena family)
H 1.5–2m July–September

The decorative fruits remain on the bush for quite some time even after the leaves have fallen. They are good to use in ornamental flower arrangements and bouquets. In terms of their colour and size they look rather like 'hundreds and thousands' that are used to decorate cakes and pastries.

4 stamens

4 flower tips

flower pink to lilac

Habitat *Native to central and western China. As ornamental shrub in central Europe. The pearl-like fruits remain on the bush over winter.*

> loose, upright growth
> can freeze right back in cold winters
> flowers attract bees and bumblebees

margin finely toothed

often with reddish veins and stalk

elliptical leaf, up to 12cm long

opposite leaves

fruit in thick clusters, about 4mm in size

Weigela
Weigela varieties (honeysuckle family)
H 1–3m May–June

5 flower tips

Nurseries offer many varieties of Weigela, which are all very easy to maintain, but nevertheless require sufficient sunshine in order to flower abundantly. They are extremely easy to propagate through cuttings. Some varieties even produce a second less profuse flowering in autumn.

funnel-shaped flower

Habitat *Originally from eastern Asia. Many varieties in parks and gardens of Europe. Flower colours vary according to variety.*

> opposite leaves
> beautiful flowering shrub
> many varieties with white to dark red flowers

flowers situated close together

thin branches, often overhanging

leaf up to about 10cm long

serrated margin

downy underside

Beautybush

Kolkwitzia amabilis (honeysuckle family)
H 2–3m May–June

withered remains of calyx

bristly fruit

overhanging branches

Habitat *Native to China. Common ornamental shrub in gardens and parks of Europe. Distinctive flowers in dense clusters.*

> hardy, easy to maintain
> grows in sun and partial shade

It is hard to believe that this wonderful ornamental shrub only arrived in Europe around 1900 and that it was first described as 'unimpressive'. This opinion changed rapidly however, when the first shrub developed its lavish blossom. This variety is named in honour of a botanist from Berlin, whose family name stems from the town of Kolkwitz in the district of Cottbus.

dense growth, heavily branched

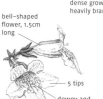

bell-shaped flower, 1.5cm long

broad oval leaf, 3–9cm long

elongated tip

opposite

5 tips

downy and patterned inside

Bodnant Viburnum

Viburnum x bodnantense (honeysuckle family)
H 2–3m October/February–March

Habitat *Only known as cultivated variety. Common in gardens and grounds in Europe. Often blossoms in snow.*

> flowers tolerate light frost
> flowers have strong sweet smell
> inconspicuous fruit

The Bodnant Viburnum came into being in the 1930s in the Bodnant Garden in Wales as a hybrid from the Fragrant Viburnum (*Viburnum farreri*) and the Himalayan Viburnum (*Viburnum grandiflorum*). As an early and abundantly flowering shrub, it has quickly become a favourite for gardens.

usually with prolific flowers

serrated margin

elongated ellip-tical leaf, up to 10cm long, dark red in autumn

long corolla tube

flower 1cm across

dense branches stretching upwards

upright growth

Wayfaring Tree

Viburnum lantana (honeysuckle family)
H 2–5m April–May

opposite leaves

Unlike the majority of other woody plants, the Wayfaring Tree has bare winter buds without any bud scales. The leaflets are easily recognisable and are protected only by a downy felt. At one time, farmers were accustomed to use the very tough, young twigs to bind together hay bales and sheaves of grain.

Habitat *Wild in central and southern Europe in copses. Planted on embankments and in gardens. Forms curved flower clusters, up to 10cm in width.*

> *flowers have unpleasant smell*
> *tolerates dryness*
> *very undemanding*

broad upright form

flattened oval fruit, 7–9mm in size

colour ranges from red to black

oval leaf, up to 12cm long

finely serrated margin

underside with thick greyish–brown down

217

Japanese Snowball

Viburnum plicatum (honeysuckle family)
H 1.5–3m May–June

There are many different hybrid varieties of the Japanese Snowball, which are all attractive ornamental shrubs. They are particularly distinctive because of their form, flowers, fruit and autumn colouring. In gardens, they require relatively moist, slightly acidic soils. They are not suited to very alkaline subsoil.

inner flowers smaller than 0.5cm in size

Habitat *Originates in China, Japan and Taiwan. In gardens and parks of Europe. Flowers often sterile in spherical clusters.*

> *flowers over a long period of time*
> *fruit red at first, black when ripe*
> *autumn leaves brownish–violet*

often with masses of fruit

outer flowers sterile, up to 4cm across

branches protrude with horizontal growth, almost tier-like in formation

serrated margin

broadly oval, slightly wavy leaf, up to 10cm long

dense growth

Black Currant

Ribes nigrum (gooseberry family)
H 1–2m April–May

remains of calyx

black berry, about 1cm in diameter

Habitat *Only rarely found wild in riverside woodlands, especially in central and northern Europe. Commonly cultivated as a fruit-bearing bush. Fruit usually ripens at different times.*

> **leaves smell extremely aromatic when crushed**
> **underside of leaf with stomata**
> **branches without thorns**

This bush can smell pleasantly aromatic or foul depending on your opinion and preference. The fruit contains fruit acids, minerals and vitamin C and is especially used for juice or Black Currant liqueur. In the 18th and 19th century, the leaves of the Black Currant bush produced a significant alternative to black and green tea which was at that time either in short supply or very expensive.

long branches, sparsely twigged

broad, outspreading growth

bell-shaped flower cupule

flowers in clusters

small, brownish petals

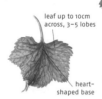

leaf up to 10cm across, 3–5 lobes

heart-shaped base

Red Currant

Ribes rubrum (gooseberry family)
H 1–2m April–May

some varieties with white berries

Habitat *Only rarely found wild in riverside woodlands of central and western Europe. Different garden varieties. Fruit hangs in long clusters.*

> **fruit ripens around St. John's Day (24th June)**
> **berries aid digestion**

The Red Currant is one of our tangiest native fruits. When removing the currants from their stalks, the fruit acid they contain can clean your hands in the exactly the same way as a lemon does. The red currants taste particularly delicious mixed with raspberries or other fruits in jam or sorbets. They are also an important ingredient of 'Cumberland Sauce'.

many projecting, sparsely branched twigs

base mainly with pointed corners

raised lip

5 greenish-yellow petals

leaf up to 8cm broad, 3–5 lobes

berries mainly red, translucent

Gooseberry

Ribes uve-crispa (gooseberry family)
H 0.5–1.5m April–May

indistinctive flowers,
greenish or brownish-red

all branches
with thorns

The majority of varieties of Gooseberry bushes came into existence after the Second World War, when food was scarce and the native fruit bushes became more and more popular. Depending on the variety, the berries taste aromatically acidic or sweet. There is also a hardy hybrid of gooseberries and blackcurrants, known as the 'Jostaberry'.

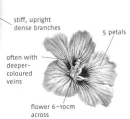

Habitat *Wild nearly all over Europe, in southern and mountainous regions. Commonly as garden fruit bush. Fruit yellow, green or reddish, depending on variety.*

> favourite fruit for healthy diet regimes in springtime
> many cultivated varieties also often cultivated as long stemmed bush

broad,
bushy growth

berries hang
individually

1–3 adjacent
thorns

tip with re-
mains of calyx

leaf 1–6cm across,
3–5 lobes

crenate margin

Syrian Ketmia

Hibiscus syriacus (mallow family)
H 1.5–2m July–September

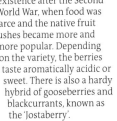

opens up
with flaps

oval-
shaped
fruit

The common name and its scientific equivalent *syriacus* would seem to imply that this shrub originates from Syria. However even in the Middle East it is an ornamental shrub that was introduced there from eastern Asia. It became known in central Europe from the end of the 16th century. It was kept in pots and then in orangeries over winter.

Habitat *Originates from eastern Asia. In gardens in central and western Europe. Noticeable because of its large, individual flowers.*

> only appropriate for areas with mild winters
> requires plenty of sun
> countless varieties with different flower colours

stiff, upright
dense branches

5 petals

leaf 5–10cm
long, 3 lobes

often with
deeper-
coloured
veins

flower 6–10cm
across

margin roughly
serrated

Castor Oil Plant
Ricinus communis (spurge family)
H 0.5–4m February–October

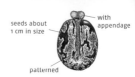

seeds about 1 cm in size

with appendage

patterned

Habitat Native to the African Tropics. Ornamental shrub in southern and central Europe, occasionally naturalised. Fruit more distinctive than flowers.

> grows very rapidly
> requires warmth
> poisonous!

In its native environment, the Castor Oil Plant grows to a height of up to 12m, in the Mediterranean it remains smaller and shrub-like. In Europe, it is normally cultivated as an annual plant. The seeds are pressed to give fatty castor oil. Even since ancient times, this oil has been used to counteract constipation. Nowadays, it is used in the cosmetic industry as it makes the skin soft and smooth.

white flowers with red stigmas

palmately lobed leaf blade

male flowers with distinctive stamens

long leaf stalk

upright branches

leaves noticeably large, often tinged red

fruit capsules with soft spines

Did you know?
Apart from their valuable oil, the seeds also contain ricin, a highly toxic substance. Eating a single seed can be fatal. Even when the seeds are worn as a necklace, the poison can still enter the body through small sores in the skin.

Whitethorn

Crataegus monogyna (rose family)
H 2–6m May–June

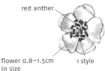

red anther

flower 0.8–1.5cm
in size
1 style

densely
branched growth,
often irregular

The Whitethorn was described as a healing plant as long ago as the days of Dioscurides, one of the most important healers in the ancient world. In the Middle Ages, herbalists recommended the fruit for menstrual tension and diarrhoea. The extremely hard kernel was also believed to prevent kidney and gall stones. The cardiotonic effect, which is still significant today, was only recognised later on.

Habitat *Wild nearly all over Europe in sunny hedgerows, woods, bushes and on rocks. Flowers appear after leaves.*

> branches have thorns
> recognised healing plant
> usually flowers later than the English Midland Hawthorn

one to multiple
stems

red one-
seeded
fruit, up to
1cm in size

leaf with 3–7
centrally indented
lobes

English Midland Hawthorn

Crataegus laevigata (rose family)
H 2–10m May–June

Medicine containing extracts of the English Midland Hawthorn are among some of the most commonly sold herbal remedies. These help alleviate heart-related problems such as mild cases of high blood pressure and circulatory problems. No matter whether the leaves, flowers or fruit is used for their healing properties, they need to be applied for at least six weeks to achieve maximum effect.

thorny branches,
squarrose twigs

Habitat *Wild nearly all over Europe in deciduous forests, hedgerows and copses. Mainly on alkaline soils. Brilliant red fruit contains two or three seeds.*

> branches have thorns
> flowers have unpleasant smell
> fruits have mealy flesh

red
anther

very
irregular
form

2 or 3
styles

flower about
1.5cm across

oval leaf, with
3–5 rounded lobes,
indented but not as far
as centre

Purple Flowering Raspberry

Rubus odoratus (rose family)
H 1.5–2m June–August

broad partially spherical, aggregate red fruit

Unlike the Wild Raspberry (p. 227) and its various varieties of cultivated garden fruit, the Purple Flowering Raspberry produces inedible fruit.
It does, however, make a decorative ornamental bush in partially shaded, slightly moist locations. However, its underground runners mean that it can become very widespread.

Habitat *Native to North America on woodland margins and stony slopes. In grounds and parks of Europe. Forms pink flowers up to 5 cm across.*

> **stalks with stiff downy hairs**
> **flowers have pleasant smell**

large leaves

broad, dense growth

mostly old, withered stems visible

leaf up to 30cm in size, with 3–5 lobes

heart-shaped base

Double Flowering Almond Tree

Prunus triloba (rose family)
H 1.5–3m March–May

flower up to 3cm across

rosette-like, nearly always densely filled, double flower

Habitat *Only as cultivated variety from China. In gardens of Europe. Characteristic double, pink flowers.*

> **usually with unlobed, elliptical leaves**
> **flowers before or with foliage**
> **only rarely produces fruit**

In contrast to the Almond Tree (p. 107), the Double Flowering Almond Tree is mainly a decorative tree. Its beautiful blossoms only emerge in their full glory in warm locations around central Europe, as the flowers are very susceptible to late frost. As well as the shrub varieties, there are also grafted varieties with trunks.

leaf up to 8cm long, 3 lobes

serrated margin

dense bushy growth

mostly heavily branched

Guelder Rose

Viburnum opulus (honeysuckle family)

H 2–4m May–June

The flowers on the edge of each cluster are infertile, but are so conspicuous that they attract insects to the small, fertile central flowers. Cultivated varieties also have dense or double flower heads, which are only made up of large flowers and look like snowballs. The birds only eat the fruit in times when food is scarce and therefore the fruit often remains on the bush until springtime. The fruit can cause diarrhoea, vomiting, nausea and mouth-burning sensations and is not for human consumption.

Habitat *Wild all over Europe in riverside woodlands, hedgerows, on woodland margins and by streams. Flower clusters up to 10cm across*

> *opposite leaves*
> *cut twigs have pleasant smell*
> *leaf stalk has glands*

Did you know?

The Guelder Rose is often easier to recognise by perforations on the foliage, as the leaves are often eaten-away and more noticeable than the flowers or fruit. The larvae of the Viburnum Leaf Beetle (Pyrrhalta viburni) are responsible for this – they are very difficult to detect.

leaf stalk mostly with 2 glands

leaf with 3 – 5 lobes

223

irregular form, often wide-spreading

central flowers indistinctive

edge flowers up to 2.5cm in size

flower clusters appear after leaves

fruit about 1cm in size

from August onwards, red and juicy

variety with spherical flower clusters

Oregon Grape

Mahonia aquifolium (barberry family)

H 0.5–1.5m April–May

Habitat *Ornamental shrub originating from western North America, occasionally naturalised. Flowers in distinctive, dense clusters.*

> **inside of bark coloured yellow, like the wood**
> **grows in sunny and shady locations**
> **also thrives in industrial areas**

odd-pinnate leaf

5–11 oval-shaped leaflets

margin with prickly teeth

upright branches

The berries act as winter food for Blackbirds and other songbirds. They distribute the seeds in their excrement and so contribute to an increase of this shrub in the wild. In humans, large quantities of the raw fruit can cause nausea and high temperatures. However, once they are cooked and sieved, the fruits are ideal for jam and quark recipes as they serve as a colouring and acidic, gelling agent.

evergreen, leathery leaves

yellow flowers, about 1cm across, in dense clusters

pruinose fruit about 8mm in size, from August onwards purple–black, bluish

224

Shrubby Cinquefoil

Potentilla fruticosa (rose family)

H 0.4–1.2m May–September

Habitat *Wild in mountains of the northern hemisphere, but only rarely in Europe. Commonly planted in gardens and green sites. Flowers mainly on end of twigs.*

> **also suitable for low hedges**
> **attracts bees**
> **also red or white flowering varieties**

The Shrubby Cinquefoil actually takes its name from the shape of its leaves. With the majority of its family members, they are in fact in the shape of a hand with five leaflets. On the Shrubby Cinquefoil, the leaves are pinnate, but nearly always with five parts. These shrubs are extremely easy to maintain and flower over a long period of time – not surprising then, that they are popular to plant.

mostly broad form, sometimes also semi-circular to spherical

very densely branched

elongated leaf with silky down

mostly 5–7 pinnate leaflets

flowers up to 4cm across

5 mostly yellow petals

Dog Rose
Rosa canina (rose family)
H 1–3m June–July

The sweet-smelling flowers are eyecatching, and the fruit or rose hips produce aromatic, pleasantly sharp-tasting tea and jam that is rich in vitamin C. Among the Germanic tribes, the Dog Rose was dedicated to the goddess of love, Frigg. It also symbolised continued life of the soul after death.

Habitat *Wild all over Europe in hedgerows, on wood margins and waysides, on wasteland. Flowers of the shrub can be white or pink*

> **fragrant flowers**
> **thorns help the plant to climb**
> **popularly used as grafted rootstock for ornamental roses**

Did you know?
Conspicuous, spherical formations tend to grow repeatedly on dog roses. These are in fact galls, the interior of which is eaten by the larvae of the Gall Wasp (Rhodites rosae) that later then pupates.

5–7 pinnate leaflets

bare leaflet, often bluish-green

225

flowers 4–5cm across

petals mainly light pink, slightly heart-shaped

slim, oval, smooth fruit

abundant stamens

sickle-shaped or hooked thorn

variable form, often wide-spreading

overhanging or also climbing branches

Redleaf Rose

Rosa glauca (rose family)
H 1–3m June–July

Habitat *Wild in the mountains of central and southern Europe, on rocks and in dry undergrowth. Bright flowers stand out between the dark foliage.*

- ***a wild rose with particularly distinctive leaves***
- ***only with some thorns***
- ***also called 'Shrub Rose'***

leaf blue-green or copper red, bluish pruinose
serrated margin
leaf with 5–7 pinnate leaflets

The roots of the Redleaf Rose can penetrate deep into rock crevices and therefore take in sufficient moisture from seemingly dry locations. Because of its deeply contrasting flowers and distinctive leaf colour, this shrub has managed to find its way into gardens as an ornamental rose. It is also popularly planted on roadside embankments because of its undemanding nature.

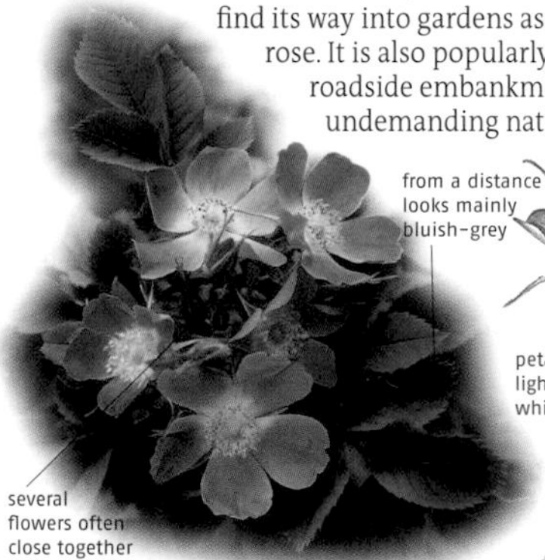
several flowers often close together
from a distance looks mainly bluish-grey

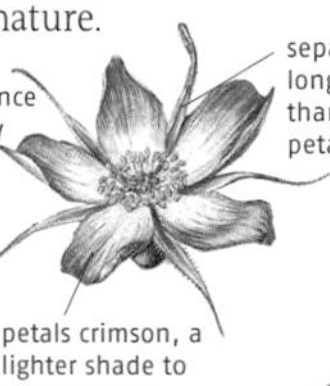
sepals longer than petals
petals crimson, a lighter shade to white below

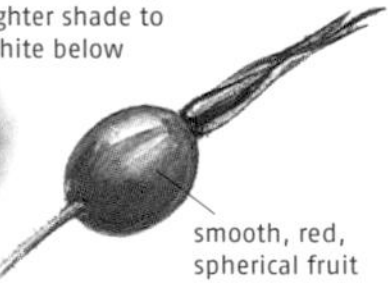
smooth, red, spherical fruit

Sweet Briar

Rosa rubiginosa (rose family)
H 1–3m June–July

Habitat *Wild all over Europe in undergrowth on infertile fields, on woodland margins, rocky slopes. Orange-coloured fruit with stalked glands.*

- ***easily recognisable by fragrance***
- ***prefers warm locations***
- ***fruit suitable for tea***

underside slightly downy and covered with red-brown stomata
leaf with 5–7 pinnate leaflets

The Sweet Briar exudes a distinct fragrance of fresh apples in early summer and also when it is rubbed. The popular saying – 'a rose between two thorns' – should really be, in botanical terms: 'No rose without prickly spines'! These spiky and defensive formations are constituted from a top membrane layer on the branch and can simply be pushed back without causing any damage to the branch. Therefore, they are nothing but a nuisance.

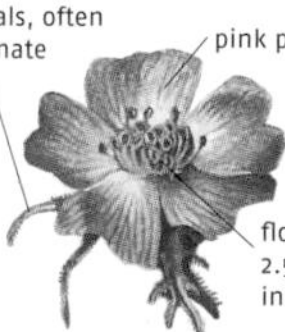
sepals longer than petals, often pinnate
pink petals
flower 2.5–4cm in size

squat form, densely branched
branches upright at first, later curved downwards and overhanging

Rugosa Rose

Rosa rugosa (rose family)
H 1–2.5m June–September

The large fruits produce considerably more fruit flesh than the Dog Rose (p. 225). They can be processed in the same way. Rose cultivators have used the Rugosa Rose as the basis of the cultivation of 'multi-flowering Shrub Roses'. Though this variety produces its main flower in June, the rest of the flowers do not appear until mid-September.

Habitat *Originates from eastern Asia. In Europe as hedge plant, on roadside embankments, on dunes, also grows wild. Characteristic flattened, spherical fruit.*

> *flowers and fruits often appear simultaneously*
> *fragrant flowers*
> *tolerates saline soils*

often forms broad undergrowth

flower mainly 6–8cm in size

petals dark pink, light pink or white

squat form

leaf with 5–9 pinnate leaflets

leaflet heavily wrinkled, shiny dark green surface

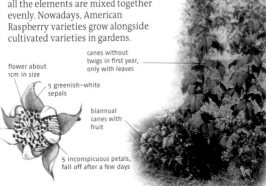

Wild Raspberry

Rubus idaeus (rose family)
H 0.5–2m May–June

red aggregate fruit

covered with style remains

The extremely flavoursome and fragrant raspberries, which are rich in vitamins, taste fresh and delicious in different sorts of culinary preparations. In tea blends, the dried downy leaves ensure that all the elements are mixed together evenly. Nowadays, American Raspberry varieties grow alongside cultivated varieties in gardens.

Habitat *Wild nearly all over Europe in forest glades, on woodland paths and rubble heaps. Unmistakeable because of its characteristic fruit.*

> *fruit is hollow in centre when picked*
> *in gardens since Middle Ages*
> *requires moist soil*

flower about 1cm in size

5 greenish–white sepals

canes without twigs in first year, only with leaves

biannual canes with fruit

5 inconspicuous petals, fall off after a few days

pinnate leaf with 3–7 leaflets

white down on underside of leaflet

with stipules at base

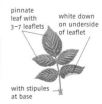

shiny black aggregate fruit

Common Blackberry
Rubus fruticosus (rose family)
H 0.5–2m May–August

Habitat *Wild nearly all Europe in copses, along hedgerows, in quarries, on embankments. Fast-growing stems can creep or climb.*

> **leaves remain green throughout winter**
> **fruit is not hollow in centre when picked**
> **leaf shape, colour and hairs very variable**

The Common Blackberry is also known as the Bramble, a name that refers to its thorns. The thorns prevent the stems from slipping backwards, when they are creeping along surfaces or climbing over other plants. The leaves contain large quantities of tannic acid and fruit acids. A tea made from them alleviates diarrhoea and inflammation of the mouth's mucous membrane.

forms impenetrable thicket

abundant stamens

flower 1.5–3cm in size

5 white or reddish petals

flower clusters on end of branches

underside of leaflet with green or white down

leaf palmately compound with 3–7 leaflets

228

pruinose black-blue, composed of 5–20 aggregate fruitlets in small drupes

European Dewberry
Rubus caesius (rose family)
H 0.5–1m May–August

Habitat *Wild nearly all of Europe in riverside woodlands, hedgerows, on riverbanks, woodland margins, scrubland. Characteristic pruinose fruits.*

> **fruit is not hollow in centre when picked**
> **indicates compressed soil**
> **can be crossed with the Blackberry**

The juicy fruits of the European Dewberry taste less flavoursome and considerably more tangy than blackberries. They are, however, suitable together with other wild fruits for mixed fruit jams or even for very good liqueur. If you go blackberry picking, you should also try harvesting European Dewberries.

mostly low-lying growth, almost mat-like

thin twigs, pruinose bluish

flower 2–2.5cm in size

abundant stamens

only end leaflet stalked

both sides green

trifoliate leaf

5 white, oval petals

Spike Broom

Cytisus nigricans (pea family)
H 0.3–1.2m June–August

yellow pea flower,
about 1cm in size

If the Spike Broom is left to dry out in a plant press, it turns black. However, if hot water is poured over it or it is pressed before it has dried out, then it stays green, as this interrupts the metabolic process that is responsible for the blackening effect.

Habitat *Wild in eastern Europe, southern Alps and on sunny wood margins. Distinctive clusters with up to 100 nodding flowers.*

> *fragrant flowers*
> *requires warm locations*
> *often also grows on stony ground*

flower heads
at end of twigs

wide bushy growth

leaflet 1–2cm long,
margin entire

upright
branches

3-part leaflet

Jupiter's Beard

Anthyllis barba-jovis (pea family)
H 0.5–2m April–June

There was originally a house plant (Sempervivum) with fleshy leaves and yellow flowers called 'Jupiter's Beard'. According to a myth in the Middle Ages, it was said to resist any lightning created by Jupiter. Later the name was transferred to this silver shimmering shrub, perhaps because from a distance it is reminiscent of Jupiter's white beard.

Habitat *Wild on coastal cliffs in Mediterranean. Cultivated as ornamental shrub in southern Europe. Flower heads in clusters at end of stems.*

> *underside of leaf espe-cially with silver sheen*
> *tolerates dryness*
> *very attractive ornamental bush, though not hardy*

twigs appear
silver grey

pale yellow flowers,
about 1cm long

usually with
abundant
flower heads

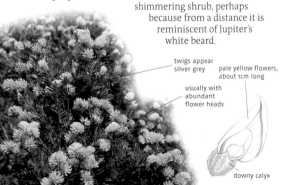

downy calyx

odd-pinnate
leaf with
13–19 leaflets

silky hairs

Siberian Peashrub
Caragana arborescens (pea family)
H 0.5–4m May–June

Habitat *Originates from Siberia and Manchuria. In Europe in parks, as wind breakers, often also on motorways. Flowers either individual or up to 4.*

> poisonous!
> undemanding on soil
> grows in sun and shade

The Siberian Peashrub was frequently planted as an ornamental shrub in gardens from the 18th century onwards. However compared to today's ornamental shrubs it does not flower very prolifically. Gardeners therefore tend to plant it in locations where low-maintenance vegetation is required as opposed to flowers.

light yellow pea flowers, about 2cm in size

cylindrical pods, 3.5–5cm long

spiny tip

abundant fruit, resembling pea pods

up to 12 pinnate leaflets, 1–2.5cm long

opened fruit with curled-up halves

Bladder-senna
Colutea arborescens (pea family)
H 1.5–4m May–August

Habitat *Wild in southern Europe. Often in central Europe in parks, gardens and on roadsides, occasionally also growing wild. Distinctive for bladder-like fruit.*

> poisonous! causes vomiting and diarrhoea
> once used as laxative
> requires warmth

The fruit remains on the shrub for a long time. In contrast to the pods of most other members of the pea family, the fruits do not open up, but are dispersed whole by the wind. If you place them on your hand and clap, they open up with a loud crack.

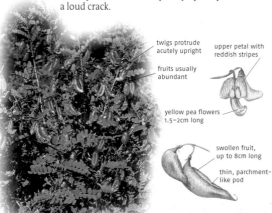

odd-pinnate leaf with 9–13 leaflets

twigs protrude acutely upright

fruits usually abundant

upper petal with reddish stripes

yellow pea flowers 1.5–2cm long

swollen fruit, up to 8cm long

thin, parchment-like pod

Japanese Bitter Orange

Poncirus trifoliata (rue family)
H 1–4m April–May

distinctive flattish thorns, up to 7cm long

In contrast to other members of its family like the Sweet Orange (p. 113) and the Lemon (p. 114), the Japanese Bitter Orange is relatively hardy, and can even be grown outside in wine-growing areas in central Europe. Gardeners often use it as a graft rootstock for the varieties of citrus which are sold as pot plants.

Habitat *Originally native to northern China. In gardens in warm areas of Europe. Fruit up to 5cm in size, remaining on branches for a long time.*

> fruit similar to oranges, but inedible
> requires plenty of sun
> decorative ornamental shrub

branches very thorny, remain green throughout the year

dense form, acutely squarrose

leaf divided into 3 parts

leathery leaflets up to 6cm long

winged stalk

Mastic Tree

Pistacia lentiscus (sumach family)
H 1–3m March–June

male flowers with red anthers

The Greeks on the island of Chios in particular cultivate tree-like specimens, to extract the Mastic resin. This is used then for Raki-Schnaps, retsina wine and to help gastric complaints. It is also used as an adhesive substance for glass and gemstones. At one time artists protected their oil paintings with a Mastic varnish, although it did turn everything a strong yellow.

small stone fruits, initially red

black when ripe

Habitat *Native to shrubland of whole of Mediterranean. Female flowers remain inconspicuous between evergreen leaves.*

> male and female shrubs
> smells like turpentine when crushed
> in the East, resin acts as chewing gum

broad form

distinctive dark green foliage throughout the year

inconspicuous female flower

pinnate leaf

8–12 leaflets

broadly winged

Turpentine Tree

Pistacia terebinthus (sumach family)
H 2–5m April–July

Habitat *Wild in whole of the Mediterranean on shrubland and in airy woodlands. Pea-sized fruit forms loose flower heads.*

> - grows as shrub, also as small tree
> - leaves only green in summer
> - occurs in the north as far as Lake Garda

odd-pinnate leaf

3–9 oval leaflets

small spike at tip

When the stem is cut into, a fragrant resin flows out, known as 'turpentine' in ancient history. Nowadays turpentine is regarded as an essential oil from the resin of pine trees. Turpentine substitute, however, came from petroleum or hard coal. In oriental countries, silk is dyed using the hollow galls frequently found on the Turpentine Tree.

female flower with red stigma

tree often bears fruit-like galls, several centimetres long

232

branches stretching upwards

loose, often broad growth

Did you know?

Green pistachios, which are the size of a hazelnut, found in baloney sausages and used for nibbles, originate from the related Pistachio (Pistacia vera). This tree is up to 10 metres tall and originates from Asia.

Bottlebrush Buckeye

Aesculus parviflora (horse-chestnut family)
H 2–4m July–August

In contrast to other members of the horse-chestnut family (p. 155 and p. 156), the Bottlebrush Buckeye always develops more than one stem. It spreads out extensively by its underground runners and, in this way, can form dense thickets. It looks its most attractive standing on its own on a large lawn. The flowers attract moths, which help with pollination.

Habitat Originates from south-eastern parts of the USA. In Europe as ornamental shrub in parks and gardens. Distinctive due to its vertical flower heads.

> flowers release fragrance in evening
> leaves turn yellow in autumn
> usually forms only few fruits, 2–3cm in size

upright branches

flower heads protrude above foliage, up to 30cm long

stamens protrude far out

white petals, about 1cm long

long and pointed

5–7 almost sessile leaflets, 8–20cm long

growth usually broader than taller

digitate leaf

233

Winter Jasmine

Jasminum nudiflorum (ash family)
H 2–3m December–April

In contrast to the related True Jasmine (see box on p. 204), the Winter Jasmine does not develop any scent. It is nevertheless a popular ornamental shrub, as its long branches hang over walls and garage roofs, thus masking any structural imperfections. In Europe, the first flowers often die off in the winter's colder temperatures, but later on the shrub is covered with flowers.

Habitat Native to mountains of northern China. Ornamental shrub in Mediterranean and central Europe. Flowers appear before foliage.

> often flowers even in snow
> inconspicuous leaves
> prefers mild situations but fairly hardy

mostly with 6 points

thin corolla tube

twigs very long and thin

flower about 2cm across

overhanging

green square twigs

trifoliate leaf

leaflet 1–3cm long, with shiny green surface

opposite

Monk's Pepper

Vitex agnus-castus (verbena family)

H 1–6m June–November

Habitat *Wild on coastlines and along river courses of the Mediterranean. Prefers warm, sunny locations. Distinctive by its abundant flower heads.*

> **strong aromatic smell when crushed**
> **also known as 'Chaste Tree'**
> **in central Europe as pot plant**

In ancient times the Greeks dedicated this shrub to Hera, the goddess of fertility, who was born beneath it, according to the legend. Even at that time, the healers knew that this plant's powers acted as an aphrodisiac. Later, it was the monks who brought the plant over to central Europe. By seasoning their meals with freshly ground, pepper-like sharp fruits, they attempted to keep their oath of celibacy and suppress their libido.

leaf divided into finger-like parts

leaflets up to 10cm long

opposite

234

flower heads up to 30cm long at end of twigs or in leaf axils

flowers with 2 lips, 6–9cm long

peppercorn-sized fruit

Did you know?

The natural substances contained within the fruit have an influence on the production of the sex hormones. Herbal remedies containing extracts from the fruit, amongst others, help counteract menstrual problems.

Bladdernut

Staphylea pinnata (bladdernut family)
H 2–5m May–June

When agitated, the seeds of the Bladdernut rattle inside the hollow fruit pods. According to an old superstition, the seeds are supposed to bring good luck. This is the reason why some people even today still carry one of these 'lucky seeds' in their purse.

Habitat Wild in southern Europe, very rarely on woodland margins in central Europe. Planted in gardens. Pea-sized seeds located inside fruit.

> lower part of shrub mostly bare
> develops characteristic fruit
> seeds once used to help potency

opposite leaves

flower heads suspended on long stalks

flowers suspended in clusters

bell-shaped flowers, 1cm long

5 elliptical pinnate leaflets, 5–10cm long

sharply serrated margin

2 or 3 points

swollen spherical fruit

235

Red Elder

Sambucus racemosa (honeysuckle family)
H 2–4m April–May

greenish yellow flowers, about 0.5cm in size

The raw sour-tasting fruit of the Red Elder can lead to sickness and diarrhoea. It was once used in medicine as a laxative and emetic. Those who enjoy experimenting with wild fruits, however, can rapidly cook the berries through, separate out the seeds and use the juice.

flowers in long, dense 8cm panicles

Habitat Wild in central Europe, native to Scandinavia. In forests, copses, on rocky slopes. Flower heads appear together with leaves.

> fruit attracts birds
> tolerates shady locations
> grows more often in mountains than on flat land

opposite leaves

fruit in dense, overhanging panicles, ripe from July onwards

bright red stone fruits, about 5mm in size

mainly 5 pinnate leaflets

sharply serrated margin

leaflet up to 8cm long

Paper Flower

Bougainvillea glabra (bougainvillea family)
H 5–8m April–September

Habitat Originates in Brazil. In southern Europe on walls and sides of buildings, in woods, in central Europe as pot plants. Distinctive for purple-red leaves.

> thorns stick out on stems
> in southern Europe, can transform walls into a sea of flowers
> very resistant to disease

The Paper Flower always has three main leaves surrounding three flowers. The yellowish flowers are, however, hardly distinguished from amidst the brightly coloured leaves. In the plant's native habitat, therefore, the leaves also attract hummingbirds to the flowers. The birds act as pollinators and are particularly attracted to the red hues of the foliage.

tubular flowers, up to 2.5cm long

3 leaves enclosing flowers

leaf oval or elongated

bare

pointed tip

climbing or shrubby growth

flowers surrounded by colourful leaves

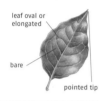

Italian Honeysuckle

Lonicera caprifolium (honeysuckle family)
H 3–6m May–July

Habitat Wild in southern Europe, in gardens of central Europe, naturalised in shrubberies. Six to 10 flowers on upper, segmented leaf pair.

> particularly fragrant in evening when flowers open up
> arrived in Europe in mid-16th century
> only flowers in sunny positions

With its dense form and almost bewitching fragrance, the Italian Honeysuckle is a popular romantic plant. In the 18th century, it was one of the most common garden plants in Europe. The flowers attract moths that hover in front of the flowers like tiny hummingbirds and locate abundant nectar in the long corolla tubes.

flower clusters stand out from foliage

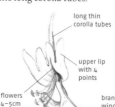

opposite leaves, bare

leaves fused at base

long thin corolla tubes

upper lip with 4 points

flowers 4–5cm long

branches wind around lower growth

Common Honeysuckle

Lonicera periclymenum (honeysuckle family)
H 3–6m May–July

bright red fruit, up to 1cm in size

The Common Honeysuckle, just like the Italian Honeysuckle (p. 236), has an extended flowering season and long climbing branches. As well as being a vigorous twiner that climbs rapidly up trellises or over arches, it is also superb trained up into trees or covering old tree stumps.

Habitat Wild in western and central Europe in deciduous woods, on wood margins, in copses. Many flowers form one head.

> leaves not fused together
> requires locations with plenty of moisture
> slightly less fragrant than Italian Honeysuckle

branches wind around base

prolific flower clusters

flower up to 6cm long

long, thin corolla tube

oval to elliptical leaf, up to 6cm long

pointed tip

mostly with stalk

Japanese Honeysuckle

Lonicera japonica (honeysuckle family)
H 2–6m May–September

The rapidly growing creeper often develops its intensive Jasmine-like fragrant flowers twice each season. The flowers are white shortly after opening and then turn yellowish later on. Some skincare products contain extracts from the leaves and flowers under the name of '*Lonicera japonica* Extract' and can soothe irritated skin.

Habitat Originates from Japan, China and Korea. Often cultivated in central and southern Europe. Flowers positioned in pairs next to each other.

blue–black fruit, 7mm in diameter, mostly in pairs

> branches hollow inside
> undemanding, tolerates heat and sun
> often grows in southern Europe over pergolas

bushy or high climbing growth

evergreen leaves or green over winter

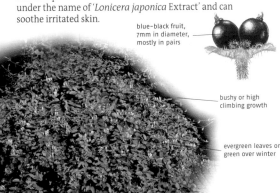

oval or elongated leaf, up to 8cm long

Russian Vine

Fallopia baldschuanica (knotweed family)

H 5–15m July–October

Habitat Trellis plant on walls, street lamps, balconies. In sunny and partially shaded locations. Attractive because of its numerous flowers.

> **winds around to left and to right**
> **undemanding and robust**
> **fragrant flowers**

This creeper was discovered in China at the end of the 19th century. It appeared in European gardens after the First World War. Very appropriately, because of its growth pattern, it was commonly known in Germany as 'Climbing Max' – after the nickname of a notorious cat burglar, who was up to mischief in Berlin in the 1920s. This plant grows rapidly and rampantly over bushes and other climbing plants.

creamy-white flowers, up to 1cm long

winged

margin slightly crenate, often wavy

elongated oval leaf

usually flowering prolifically

shoots only become woody after many years

one single plant can cover large areas

Did you know?

The Russian Vine can grow several metres in a year and so provides quick coverage for house walls, concealing structural imperfections and bare concrete walls. For this reason it is also popularly planted on sound barriers.

Kiwifruit
Actinidia deliciosa (dogbane family)
H 5–7m June

The Kiwifruit began its triumphal entry into Europe in the 1960s. To start with, the fruit came mainly from New Zealand's cultivating areas, but today it is widely cultivated in the countries of the Mediterranean. The fruit is rich in vitamin C as well as an enzyme that destroys protein. Therefore, raw kiwifruit should not be mixed with dairy products.

Habitat *Originates initially from China. Cultivated in the Mediterranean, rarely in central Europe. Fruit only ripens in warm European summers.*

> **underside of leaf with thick, grey down**
> **fragrant flowers**
> **male and female plants**

abundant stamens

dense foliage

fruit concealed under leaves

5 petals

creamy-white flowers, mainly 3–5cm in size

tip mainly pointed

finely serrated margin

broad oval, coarse, thick leaf, 8–12cm long

239

Climbing Hydrangea
Hydrangea anomala ssp. *petiolaris* (mockorange family)
H 2–15m July

The Climbing Hydrangea grips the soil below ground with its firm roots and in doing so, climbs up walls. However, the flowering branches are often so heavy that a strong wind can break them loose from the wall. If the firm anchoring roots disturb the ground, they develop into normal roots. Young plants can grow up again from these root-like branches.

Habitat *Originates from Japan, Korea and Taiwan. Cultivated in Europe. Umbrella-shaped flower clusters up to 25cm in size with enlarged flowers on edge.*

> **grows relatively slowly**
> **large flowers on edge stay attractive over many weeks**
> **also flowers in shady locations**

no leaves with opened flowers

very dense growth

small inner flowers

flower clusters stand out from foliage

very long leaf stalk

roundish leaf, up to 10cm long

Grape Vine
Vitis vinifera (grape-vine family)
H 5–20m June–July

Habitat *Only rarely wild in riverside woodland. Cultivars planted regularly in warm regions, occasionally wild. Autumn colours yellow or red.*

> holds firm with help of tendrils
> fragrant flowers
> cultivated worldwide in many varieties

Scientists date the earliest reference to viniculture back to 3500–2900 B.C. The Grape Vine is one of the oldest cultivated plants. Grapes contain glucose, a carbohydrate, which the body rapidly absorbs into the bloodstream, providing a quick burst of energy. In addition, the fruit provides many minerals and vitamins B and C. The vast majority of fruit, however, is not eaten fresh but pressed into wine.

irregularly serrated margin

heart-shaped base

leaves with mainly 3–5 lobes

240

fruit yellowish to purplish-blue depending on variety

climbing branches

indistinctive flowers in elongated, dense panicles

hanging fruit clusters

Did you know?
Vintners have been using leaf infusions and paste-like compresses for a long time for the treatment of swollen, painful legs. Now ready-made compounds are available to counteract varicose veins and phlebitis, which contain red vine leaves.

Japanese Creeper

Parthenocissus tricuspidata (grape-vine family)
H 5–15m June–August

This attractive creeper was a big seller after its introduction to Holland over 100 years ago. It is undemanding and, unlike many other creepers, does not require any support. It can, however, sometimes grow over and into the roof of a house, thus displacing tiles. After removing the plant from a wall, some tendril-like parts remain stuck to the surface like suckers and must be painstakingly scraped or burned off.

Habitat Native to China and Japan. In Europe on outside and house walls. Tendrils with suckers enable the plant to fasten onto surfaces, even smooth ones.

> *bare in winter*
> *tolerates even polluted urban air*
> *fruit slightly poisonous*

on young shoots, leaves almost unlobed

shiny green leaf

toothed margin

mainly 3 lobes

dark blue berry fruit, pruinose

241

flat narrow climber, creeps close to surface

Did you know?
Walls covered in Japanese Creeper gleam bright red in autumn and thus are distinctive from a distance.

English Ivy
Hedera helix (ivy family)
H 0.5–20m September–October

Habitat *Wild almost all over Europe in woods, on rocks and ruins. Planted on walls, in gardens and parks. Flowers develop in autumn.*

> *suitable as green coverage for walls*
> *many cultivated varieties*
> *fruit acts as food for birds in spring*

The English Ivy grows towards the light with the aid of anchoring roots, which fix onto stones and stems. In ancient history ivy was dedicated to the Gods of Wine, acting as a symbol of cheerfulness and conviviality. Eminent poets were once honoured with an ivy wreath. In the Christian faith, the evergreen ivy is seen as a sign of eternal life. This is why people like to plant it on graves and chisel its leaf shape onto gravestones.

greenish yellow flowers, about 0.5cm in size

leaves of flowering branches are unlobed, diamond-shaped

evergreen leathery leaf, with 3–5 lobes

242

blue–black fruit, up to 1cm wide

dense foliage

climbing branches

Did you know?
The English Ivy is no parasite. Instead, it is self-sufficient and finds its own source of nutrients. If it develops too prolifically in the crown of a tree, however, the tree can 'suffocate' or collapse under its weight.

forms stems with anchoring roots

Old Man's Beard

Clematis vitalba (buttercup family)

H 5–15m June–September

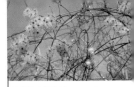

The flowers attract bees and flies with their unpleasant smell. The fruit does not ripen until winter and only breaks off the parent plant in strong winds. From the 16th to the 19th century, Old Man's Beard was also planted in gardens, particularly for green coverage for bowers. Nowadays, there are more attractive clematis plants that are suited to this purpose, with larger and brightly coloured flowers.

Habitat *Wild in central and southern Europe in riverside glades, on woodland margins, on wasteland. Fruit particularly distinctive in winter.*

> *sap irritates the skin*
> *indicates nitrogen-rich soil*
> *can spread over wide areas*

obscures plant support almost entirely with its winding stem

dense leaves

fruit with long, feathery, downy style

flowers up to 2.5cm in size

odd-pinnate leaf with 3 or 5 long, stalked leaflets

4 early-dropping petals

abundant stamens

stalk often crooked or coiled

243

Alpine Clematis

Clematis alpina (buttercup flower)

H 1–3m May–July

The Alpine Clematis is protected in its natural habitat. However, nurseries offer different garden varieties for sale. Fresh clematis plants contain a poisonous, sharp, burning sap. This irritates the skin so much so that blisters can form. Beggars often used to rub it on their skin, intentionally, in order to gain sympathy.

Habitat *Wild in the mountains of central and southern Europe and in Lapland. Develops wig-like fruit.*

> *suspended flowers*
> *requires moist ground*
> *also suitable for gardens*

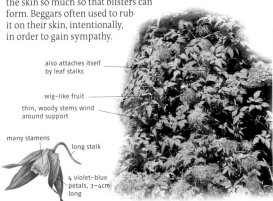

also attaches itself by leaf stalks

wig-like fruit

thin, woody stems wind around support

many stamens

long stalk

4 violet-blue petals, 3–4cm long

double trifoliate leaf

roughly serrated leaflet up to 5cm long

Chinese Wisteria
Wisteria sinensis (pea family)
H 8–10m May–June

Habitat *Originates from China.*
Cultivated in warm, sunny locations on walls, pergolas and balconies. Individual flowers of clusters open simultaneously.

> **entire plant is poisonous, especially seeds!**
> **flowers have strong fragrance**
> **bare in winter**

In China the stems of the Chinese Wisteria growing in the wild coil around trees and obscure hedges. Gardeners in these locations were planting this variety for a long time as a decorative ornamental plant before the first living specimen arrived in Europe in 1816. It is not worth cultivating young plants from seed, as they often do not bear their first flowers for over 10 years. It is better to acquire more plants by separating the runners it forms.

flowers about 2.5cm in size

violet-blue pea flowers

odd-pinnate leaf

7–13 oval elongated leaflets

climbing shrub with stems winding to left

long flower panicles up to 30cm long appear before leaves

244

Did you know?

On ripening, the lower part of the fruit pod, which is up to 15cm long, opens with an explosive action, flinging the seeds out for distances of up to 9m.

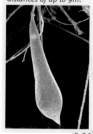

requires climbing support on walls

Virginia Creeper

Parthenocissus quinquefolia (grape-vine family)
H 8–15m June–August

This undemanding climber came to Europe around 1610 and was used early on in parks as green coverage for arcades. However, unlike the Japanese Creeper (p. 241), it cannot attach itself as well to house walls. It is therefore better planted on trellises that it can wind around with its tendrils.

indistinctive flowers in loose panicles

Habitat Originates from North America. In Europe on fences, pergolas and houses, occasionally also naturalised. Shoots frequently tinged red.

> also known as 'Virginia Vine'
> grows very rapidly
> prefers sun, but also tolerates shade

leaves turn red in autumn

dense foliage

leaf mainly palmate with 5 parts

climbs with tendrils

roughly serrated margin

long stalk

Yellow Trumpet Tree

Campsis radicans (bignonia family)
H 5–10m July–September

climber reaching height of up to 10m

overhanging flowering shoots

In its native environment this plant attracts hummingbirds. They hover in front of the flowers and stick their heads as far inside as possible to retrieve the sugary nectar that is hidden in the flower tubes. In Europe we often see wasps on the flowers. They climb around outside the calyx, where they also seem to find nectar.

Habitat Originates from the USA. Decorative plant in Europe on walls and balconies in sunny locations. Flowers formed in horizontal clusters.

> climbs with aid of anchoring roots
> also as a variety with yellow flowers
> hardy

clusters of flowers at end of shoots

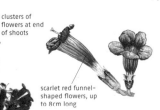

scarlet red funnel-shaped flowers, up to 8cm long

odd-pinnate leaf

toothed margin

9–11 leaflets

Index of Species

Index of Species

Index of Species

Illustrations and Photographs

Illustrations
M. Golte-Bechtle/Kosmos (476); S. Haag/Kosmos (29); R. Hofmann/Kosmos (11); G. Kohnle/Kosmos (2); W. Lang/Kosmos (3); R. Spohn/Kosmos (351)

Photographs
A. Bärtels 39aM, 43bM, 58bM, 66aM, 67M, 74aM, 86bM, 93M, 95aM, 108bM, 113M, 114aM, 142M, 143aM, 156bM, 156bS, 229bM; D. Smit 64aM; H.E. Laux 222bM; M. Pforr 70bM, 237aM; R. Spohn 2, 16/17, 18M, 18B, 18S, 18E4, 19aM, 19aS, 19bM, 19bS, 20aM, 20aS, 20bM, 20bS, 21M, 21B, 21S, 22aM, 22aS, 22bM, 22bM, 22bE2, 23M, 23B, 23S, 24aM, 24aS, 24bM, 24bS, 25M, 25B, 25S, 26aM, 26aS, 26bM, 26bS, 27aM, 27aS, 27bM, 27bS, 28aM, 28aS, 28bM, 28bS, 29M, 29S, 30M, 30B, 30S, 31aM, 31aS, 31bM, 31bS, 32M, 32B, 32S, 33aM, 33aS, 33bM, 33bS, 34M, 34B, 34S, 35aM, 35aS, 35bM, 35bS, 36M, 36B, 36S, 37M, 37B, 37S, 38M, 38B, 38S, 39aS, 39bM, 39bS, 39bE2, 40M, 40S, 41aM, 41aS, 41bM, 41bS, 42M, 42B, 42S, 43aM, 43aS, 43bS, 43bE, 44M, 44B, 44S, 44E3, 45aM, 45aS, 45bM, 45bS, 45bE, 46M, 46B, 46S, 47aM, 47aS, 47bM, 47bS, 48M, 48B, 48S, 49aM, 49aS, 49bM, 49bS, 50M, 50B, 50S, 51aM, 51aS, 51bM, 51bS, 52M, 52B, 52S, 53aM, 53aS, 53bM, 53bS, 54M, 54B, 54S, 55aM, 55aS, 55bM, 55bS, 56M, 56B, 56S, 57M, 57B, 57S, 58aM, 58aS, 58bS, 59aM, 59aS, 59bM, 59bS, 60M, 60B, 60S, 60E1, 61aM, 61aS, 61bM, 61bS, 62M, 62B, 62S, 63aM, 63aS, 63bM, 63bS, 64aS, 64aE, 64bM, 64bS, 65M, 65B1, 65B2, 65S, 66aS, 66bM, 66bS, 67B, 67S, 68M, 68S, 68E2, 69aM, 69aS, 69bM, 69bS, 70aM, 70aS, 70bS, 71M, 71B, 71S, 72aM, 72aS, 72bM, 72bS, 73M, 73B, 73S, 74aS, 74bM, 74bS, 75M, 75B, 75S, 76M, 76B, 76S, 77aM, 77aS, 77bM, 77bS, 78M, 78B, 78S, 79aM, 79aS, 79bM, 79bS, 80M, 80B, 80S, 81aM, 81aS, 81bM, 81bS, 82M, 82B, 82S, 83aM, 83aS, 83bM, 83bS, 84M, 84B, 84S, 84E, 85M, 85B, 85S, 85E3, 86aM, 86aS, 86aS, 87M, 87B, 87S, 88aM, 88aS, 88bM, 88bS, 88bE1, 89M, 89B, 89S, 90aM, 90aS, 90aE, 90bM, 90bS, 91M, 91B, 91S, 91E2, 92aM, 92aS, 92bM, 92bS, 93B, 93S, 94M, 94B, 94S, 94E2, 95aS, 95bM, 95bS, 96aM, 96aS, 96bM, 96bS, 97M, 97B, 97S, 98aM, 98aS, 98bM, 98bS, 99aM, 99aS, 99bM, 99bS, 100M, 100B, 100S, 100E1, 101aM, 101aS, 101bM, 101bS, 102aM, 102aS, 102bM, 102bS, 103M, 103B, 103S, 104aM, 104aS, 104bM, 104bS, 105M, 105B, 105S, 105E2, 106M, 106B, 106S, 107M, 107B, 107S, 107E3, 108aM, 108aS, 108bS, 109M, 109B, 109S, 110M, 110B, 110S, 111aM, 111aS, 111aE2, 111bM, 111bS, 112aM, 112aS, 112bM, 112bS, 113B, 113S, 114aS, 114bM, 114bS, 115M, 115B, 115S, 115E4, 116M, 116B, 116S, 116E1, 117M, 117S, 118M, 118S, 119aM, 119aS, 119aE3, 119bM, 119bS, 120M, 120S, 121aM, 121aS, 121bM, 121bS, 122aM, 122B, 122S, 123aM, 123aS, 123bM, 123bS, 124M, 124B, 124S, 125M, 125B, 125S, 126aM, 126aS, 126bM, 126bS, 127M, 127S, 128M, 128B, 128S, 129aM, 129aS, 129bM, 129bS, 130aM, 130aS, 130bM, 130bS, 131aM, 131aS, 131bM, 131bS, 132M, 132B, 132S, 133aM, 133aS, 133bM, 133bS, 134aM, 134aS, 134bM, 134bS, 134bE2, 135M, 135S, 135E1, 136aM, 136aS, 136bM, 136bS, 137M, 137B, 137S, 138aM, 138aS, 138bM, 138bS, 139M, 139B, 139S, 139E2, 140aM, 140aS, 140bM, 140bS, 141M, 141B, 141S, 141E2, 142B, 142S, 143aS, 143bM, 143bS, 144M, 144S, 145aM, 145aS, 145bM, 145bS, 146M, 146B, 146S, 147M, 147B, 147S, 148aM, 148aS, 148aE, 148bM, 148bS, 149M, 149B, 149S, 149E3, 150aM, 150aS, 150bM, 150bS, 151M, 151B1, 151B2, 151S, 151E3, 152aM, 152aS, 152bM, 152bS, 153M, 153B, 153S, 154aM, 154bS, 154bS, 154bS, 154bE2, 155M, 155B, 155S, 156aM, 156aS, 156bE2, 157M, 157B, 157S, 158aM, 158aS, 158bM, 158bS, 159aM, 159aS, 159bS, 159bE, 160aM, 160aS, 160bM, 160bS, 161aM, 161aS, 161bM, 161bS, 162M, 162B, 162S, 163aM, 163aS, 163bM, 163bS, 164M, 164B, 164S, 165M, 165B, 165S, 165E2, 166M, 166B, 166S, 167aM, 167aS, 167bM, 167bS, 168aM, 168aS, 168bM, 168bS, 169M, 169B, 169S, 169E2, 170aM, 170aS, 170bM, 170bS, 171M, 171B, 171S, 172aM, 172aS, 172bM, 172bS, 173M, 173B, 173S, 173E2, 174aM, 174aS, 174bM, 174bS, 175M, 175B, 175S, 176aM, 176aS, 176bM, 176bS, 177M, 177B, 177S, 177E3, 178aM, 178aS, 178bM, 178bS, 179aM, 179aS, 179bM, 179bS, 180aM, 180aS, 180bM, 180bS, 181M, 181B, 181S, 182aM, 182aS, 182bM, 182bS, 182bE, 183aM, 183aS, 183bM, 183bS, 184aM, 184aS, 184bM, 184bS, 185M, 185B, 185S, 186aM, 186aS, 186bM, 186bS, 187M, 187B, 187S, 188M, 188B, 188S, 189aM, 189aS, 189bM, 189bS, 190M,

M = Main photograph, S = Small photograph, E = Extra detail, B = Box, a = above, b = below

BLACK'S NATURE GUIDES

ISBN 978 1 4081 0155 1

ISBN 978 1 4081 0153 7

ISBN 978 1 4081 0154 4

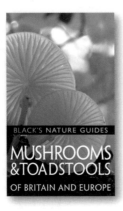

ISBN 978 1 4081 0156 8

ISBN 978 1 4081 0152 0

The new Black's nature guides – compact, concise and comprehensive

www.acblack.com